WALKER SUN BOOKS
continued

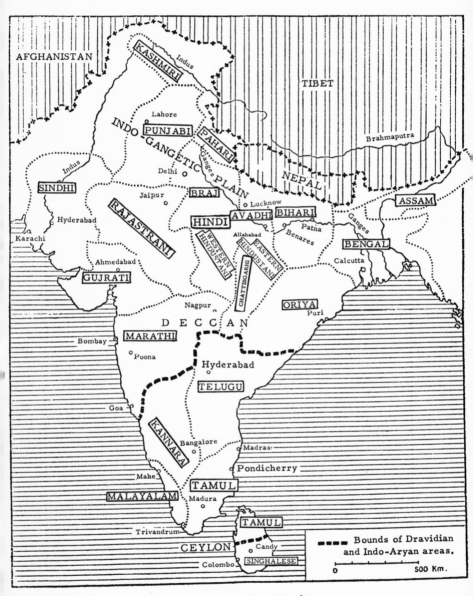

Linguistic Map of India

Indian Literature

by LOUIS RENOU
Member of the Institute

Translated from the French by Patrick Evans

/ A SUN BOOK

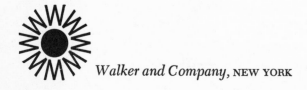

Walker and Company, NEW YORK

CONTENTS

Part Four / The Modern Indo-Aryan Literatures

Part One / Sanskrit Literature

1 THE VEDA AND THE EPIC

The Veda

The earliest literary documents of India were religious compositions handed down at first by word of mouth only. They were
eventually assembled and written down, but have always remained characteristically "oral texts," passed on from generation to generation by professional reciters. We do not know
when or by whom they were composed. But as they came into
being among the "Aryans"—that is, among people of Indo-European origin who had invaded northwest India probably about
2000 B.C.—we must conclude that the most ancient of the Vedic
texts go back to that period; they may have been written down
rather later. Moreover, this Vedic literature extends, intermit-
tently, over a considerable period; the latest authentic specimens of it may date from the sixth or fifth century B.C. or may
be more recent still.

The language of the most ancient documents is an archaic
Sanskrit (known as "Vedic Sanskrit") that resembles the Iranian

of the most ancient portions of the *Avesta* (the parts known as the *gāthās*); it is not far removed from Indo-European, the language from which both Iranian and Sanskrit descended. The morphology of Vedic Sanskrit is extremely rich and the syntax very free; as for the vocabulary, it contains a host of words whose meanings we do not know and a number of known words used in unfamiliar ways. Language is here in bondage to a system of ritualistic references; it has to express correlations between various features of worship or of the human body and mind on the one hand, and "atmospheric" and celestial phenomena on the other. Vedic worship is conceived as the imitation of the major phenomena of nature, which in turn are believed to be consequences of a primordial celestial sacrifice. These demands made on language have had a direct effect on linguistic usage; they have given rise to a symbolism that added to the desire of many of the "authors" of the Veda to surround themselves with an atmosphere of mystery, has made these obscure writings yet more obscure.

As the centuries passed and poetry gave way to prose, the language was brought within narrower bounds, and style became simpler. Though esoteric, like the earlier writings, the *Brâhmanas* have a rigorous syntax and a thoroughly stable vocabulary; and, in the last stage of Vedism, the *Upanishads*, contain a Sanskrit that has almost become what is known as "classical Sanskrit."

The earliest part of the literature consists of the *Samhitâs*, or "Collections," which form the essential portion of what was originally called the "Three Vedas" (the word means "knowledge, [sacred] lore"), or "the Triple Knowledge"; a fourth group of writings was admitted later and the whole then became known as the "Four Vedas."

The contents of these collections show considerable variety. The first Veda, the oldest and most important, the *Rig-Veda*, or "Veda of the stanzas," comprises about a thousand hymns to the deities, arranged in a fairly strict and systematic way; the meter of some of these hymns is not unlike that of certain Greek lyrics. This Veda also includes a few pieces of a semi-profane kind, poems in dialogue, cosmogonic hymns and so on, but the greater part of it is dedicated to the major deities: either to those who were the dominant figures in worship, such as Agni, god of fire, and Soma, the sacrificial liquor; or else to those who protected and insured the results of worship, such as Indra, the warrior god, Varuna, the dispenser of temporal power, the Ashvins (the Indian Dioscuri) and a number of others.[1] The composition of the hymns is governed by precise rules. There is a prescribed method for composing a panegyric to a god and for recalling (without describing them) his mythical exploits; there is another for introducing allusions to the sacrificial ritual; finally, the poets had ingenious ways of introducing, often in veiled terms, a eulogy of their patrons and of asking favors and worldly advantages both on their patrons' behalf and their own.

Viewed as a whole, this body of poetry leaves a certain impression of monotony, especially since the phraseology is often identical from one piece to another, at least within any series devoted to the same deity. What used to be called henotheism, that is to say, a tendency to attach to the god one is praising the characteristics and assorted objects of other gods, intensified this stylistic unification. But for all that, the language is full of vigor, character and flavor, richly allusive and with various secondary virtues; its metaphorical equipment is highly developed, and accounts for what has been called the "confusion" of the Veda. The more highly inspired of these poems embark directly on the great themes of Indian philosophical thought, the search for unity amid diversity. As for the *Rig-Veda's* authors, their names are just so many words telling us nothing; tradition has it that they were *rishis*, inspired individuals to whom it was

[1] See Louis Renou's *The Nature of Hinduism* (New York: Walker and Company, 1962), chap. i.

granted to "see" the hymns by direct revelation from above.

The second Veda is the *Yajur-Veda,* the "Veda of sacrificial formulae." It has come down to us in different versions. Some contain only the sacrificial formulae used in the various rites of the cult, in verse or in prose. Other versions, known as the Black *Yajur-Veda* (in contradistinction to the White *Yajur-Veda),* also contain the outlines of a commentary intended to illuminate either the meaning of the formulae, or, more commonly, the significance of the various gestures and actions occurring in the ceremonial sacrifice. These are the first examples of the continuous prose known as *brâhmanas,* "reflections on the *brahman";* the meaning of the latter term, in this context, being "the formula, and the mystical force arising from it."

The third Veda, the *Sama-Veda,* or "Veda of the melodies," is, from the literary viewpoint, merely an extract from the *Rig-Veda,* with the stanzas arranged differently and in some instances provided with variants. The interest of the collection lies in the musical setting that accompanies the stanzas (the collection was a handbook of liturgical chanting). Both the setting and the verbal changes made in the spoken text to adapt it for singing are important for the history of music; for this is the oldest known liturgical music in the world.

The last Veda, which made its way into the company of the three others only with difficulty and at a comparatively late period, is the *Atharva-Veda.* This is a miscellaneous selection of poems, of which some are borrowed from the *Rik,* while a larger number are original and of a rather different type. Some of these latter are magical prayers; others are a disjointed series of texts for use in private ceremonies not carried out in temples, such as marriages and funerals; and there are also philosophical pieces on certain rarefied entities treated as the basis of an occult symbolism. The language used is often more modern than that of the *Rik,* and the style is at times less scholarly, though it is not, as some have claimed, completely "popular." The religion of the

Atharvans was connected with different social backgrounds from those associated with the *Rik;* it was linked with magicians, shamans and "strangers" of various kinds. Several of the magical prayers and cosmogonic poems are of great beauty.

The Brâhmanas and the Upanishads

The second great document of Vedic literature is the *Brâhmanas.* These are prose commentaries of the type we have already seen taking shape from the ritualistic formulae of the *Yajus,* but they now form the subject matter of special manuals and are most extensive and detailed. Some of them are attached to the different *Samhitâs* and are classified as belonging to different schools, but these schools really represent little more than different recensions of the commentaries. The *Brâhmanas* comment on the formulae and analyze some of the words occurring in them (these analyses are the beginnings of a pseudo-etymology with tendencies toward symbolism); they interpret the Vedic myths in such a way as to fix the connections between those ancient stories and the current sacrificial usages. The *Brâhmanas* are the exegesis of sacrifice; and from then on the act of sacrifice is religion's vital center. The most important of the *Brâhmanas* is the *Satapatha (-Brâhmana),* the *Brâhmana* "of the Hundred Ways"; the language is admirably austere though the thought is imprisoned within a system of classifications that is paralogical rather than logical. Many precious legends, including that of the Flood, are preserved in this *Brâhmana.*

One part of the *Brâhmanas* is esoteric: the *Aranyakas,* or "Forest Books," which were recited in lonely places. These texts give an outline of a symbolic hierarchy of ritualistic values, an outline that is subsequently amplified by the *Upanishads,* or "Treatises Relating to the Equivalences" (between microcosm and macrocosm); this is the primary meaning of the word *upanishad.* But these treatises venture out in directions that soon take them beyond the bounds of liturgical and even religious needs. At the end of their quest for "equivalences" they come to supreme identification, the "truth of all truths," the equation between the individual soul *(âtman)* and the ancient principle, at once mystical and ritualistic, of the *brahman,* which is here promoted to the rank of the universal soul. The formula that sums up this doctrine is "Thou art that": in other words, "Thou, the individual soul, art identical with That, the universal soul." This principle is illustrated by many parables and many reminders of ancient sacrificial themes, and by episodes borrowed from the discussions and controversies that took place ever more frequently among sophists and theologians, and in which even princes and women took part. The *Upanishads* hardly constitute a coherent whole, but the incomparable grandeur of certain passages has never ceased to captivate the West since Schopenhauer came into contact with them through the first European translation, made a century and a half ago: the Latin version by Anquetil Duperron of a seventeenth-century Persian translation.

The *Upanishads* take us to the very brink of Hinduism: they open the gates to the philosophical speculation of classical India at the same time as they reflect and consummate the values of the past. Now we must return to the heart of Vedism and study other texts, which, while they have no literary value in the proper sense, are of primary importance for the development of religious practice, or, in other cases, for the establishing of certain intellectual and practical techniques that were part of life in ancient India.

The Sûtras and Auxiliary Texts

The chief works in this category are the *Sûtras,* or "Aphorisms," which represent the *Kalpa,* or ritualistic doctrine. They consist of extraordinarily minute descriptions of the ceremonies of worship: daily, fortnightly and four-monthly sacrifices; occasional sacrifices (such are the Royal Consecration, and the Horse Sacrifice); votive rites, expiations and so on.[2] These ceremonies involved a more or less numerous body of officiating priests, and also the "master of the sacrifice," the layman for whose benefit the work was carried out and who footed the bill. The sections into which the descriptions are divided correspond to the persons officiating: there are manuals for the "invoker and maker of libations" (the formulae for this aspect of the sacrifice are drawn from the *Rig-Veda),* and others for the liturgical singers (whose formulae come from the *Sâma-Veda),* and, especially, manuals for the *adhvaryu,* the priest who makes most of the ritual gestures and, in an undertone, recites appropriate formulae from the *Yajus.* Each of these manuals belongs to such and such a school, which means in effect that it departs more or less widely from the basic text, the restoration of which is at once necessary and impossible.

These texts are the most important description of ritual practices from the ancient world. The rites attest a considerable degree of development in contrast with the religion whose nature can be inferred from the Vedic hymns; the religion of the *Sûtras* is much more complicated, with its alternation of vegetable offerings, libations of *soma,* and bloody sacrifices. The whole constitutes the solemn or "revealed" cult, whose origins lie in the *Rig-Veda.* But side by side with this cult there was a simpler, private ceremonial, which dispensed with the help of a professional clergy. The private rites (including the *samskâras,* or "sacraments" marking the stages in the life of the "twice-born") are described in the "Domestic Aphorisms," which, like the others, are divided into different schools. Finally, there are the "Aphorisms on the Law" *(dharma),* which incorporate, along with religious material, the beginnings of a system of civil and penal law. The prose of all these texts is more or less terse,

---

[2] Renou, *Nature of Hinduism,* chap. i.

designed for learning by heart, and difficult to understand without the help of a commentary.

There are, in addition, various other texts auxiliary to the Veda. The most remarkable among them are the treatises on phonetics (the oldest works of this kind in any literature), intended to insure the correct pronunciation of the formulae and stanzas; they are the beginnings of studies of grammar that will come to fruition later, as the period of the Vedic disciplines comes to an end. There are "aphorisms" for the building of altars and hearths (with the rudiments of a geometry); others for establishing the calendar (these include observations on astronomy); treatises on etymology and prosody; and a literature of commentaries, the production of which went on for a long time after the Vedic period. The most highly reputed commentary on the *Rig-Veda,* that of Sâyana, was written in the fourteenth century, but it inherited a tradition that goes back much further.

Born among not very powerful clans that had to insure their survival amid a hostile population and against the pressure of rival groups, Vedism gradually spread eastward, and later southward. In historical times (which, it is true, begin late in India), there are signs of the existence of the various Vedic schools in all corners of the vast territory of Indian civilization. The "creative" stream in Vedic literature came early to a stop, as if it had dried up, but religious practices derived from it insinuated themselves into classical Hindu worship; in the process some of them were changed almost beyond recognition. The Veda wielded a considerable influence on literary creation in later times, and even in our own day the texts continue to be studied, learned by heart, and recited with unparalleled accuracy; some of the Vedic ceremonies have been reconstituted in their entirety.

The Epic; The Mahâ-Bhârata

The sixth century B.C. was a period of high effervescence.

While the Vedic disciplines were dwindling away in controversies between rival schools of thought, the preaching of Buddha and that of Jina, in eastern India, began making progress both among the sophists who gathered under priestly patronage, and in groups protected by influential laymen. And at the same time, Hinduism, at first nameless and so to speak undifferentiated, began to take organic shape in the form of a vast written tradition. The origins of Hindu literature doubtless date from this period, though the great texts received their definitive form somewhat later—roughly, we may say, at the start of the Christian era. These texts are on the one hand the two Epics, and on the other the oldest treatises in the *Smriti*, or "memorized" tradition (as distinct from the "revealed" tradition, the Veda); and along with these there are the earliest documents of Purânic literature. Nothing in all this provides the canon of Hinduism, which was never formally established; indeed, most of these texts are not essentially religious. What they do, in their very diverse ways, is to set forth the Hindu *dharma*, that Law, Norm or whatever else one chooses to call it that governs the conduct of all beings not only on the plane of religion but also on those of morals, social living, the law and even health.

There is no epic period as such, as scholars used to think. The growth of epic was a marginal development: in certain privileged circles of minstrels or bards who led an eremitical life but were in contact with the *kshatriyas* ("nobility"), there took place a slow maturing of epic themes (partly inspired by the Veda) that finally resulted in the production of two great literary compilations.

Of the two Epics, the older in both inspiration and style (its linguistic basis is a Sanskrit that is still comparatively archaic) is the *Mahâ-Bhârata*, the "(Story of the) Great (War) of the Bhâratas." This is an anonymous work (the attribution to Vyâsa is fictitious); it exists in several versions, whose derivation from a single common source has been more or less convincingly established. The main narrative concerns the rivalry between two related princely families, the hundred Kauravas commanded by the barbarous Duryodhana, and five brothers who are cousins of the Kauravas, the Pândavas, who have one wife among them, the daughter of King Drupada, Draupadî, called Krishnâ "the Black One." The rivalry has originated long before the marriage: the Kauravas have succeeded in persuading the aged king Dhritarâshtra to condemn their cousins to exile. It is during this first sojourn of theirs in the forest that the cousins win Draupadî, following the success of one of them, the hero Arjuna, in bending a supernatural bow. At this, Duryodhana decides to push the conflict to a conclusion. He begins by using trickery; challenging the eldest of the brothers to a gambling contest, he takes every precaution to make sure of winning, strips his adversary of all his possessions, and proclaims his right to reduce Draupadî to slavery. The Pândavas depart once more into exile. At the end of twelve years, a period as full of adventures as any that has gone before, they return and claim the kingdom.

War is inevitable, and both camps prepare for it by forming alliances with tribes who have gathered from all over India and from a number of neighboring countries. The battle rages for eighteen days on the "Field of the Kurus," the holy land of Brahmanism (in the region of present-day Delhi); fortune favors now this side and now that, and the dead lie ever thicker on the blood-stained ground. After the clash of cohorts come single combats between heroes, who succumb one by one, Duryodhana being the last to fall. The five Pândavas survive; they even escape a final bout of slaughter perpetrated by the last living Kaurava, who makes a surprise attack when, after the battle, the armies of the Pândavas believe the field to be clear of the enemy and are consequently recuperating their energies in sleep. Some time later the Pândavas die, too, and Draupadî with them, overtaken by a supernatural death when on their way to the Himalayas.

The poem belongs to the category of epics with a tragic ending—the effect being mitigated in this case, however, by the Indian conception of destiny. The story abounds in digressions: discourses on morals, law and philosophy, fables and parables, and various episodes that have no connection with the main narrative, such as the long, independent story of *Nala and Damayantî*, the lovers who are caused to part by Nala's consuming passion for gaming; or again, the story of *Sâvitrî*, the faithful wife who wrests her dead husband from the talons of the god Yama.

The characters of the protagonists are powerfully drawn. The most curious among them is that of the hero Krishna, the Pândavas' cousin and ally, who contributes to their victory by means that are sometimes extremely underhanded. This clan chieftain reveals himself as a supreme god[3] at the end of the teaching that, on the eve of the battle, he imparts to Arjuna, both to encourage the latter to fight and to provide him with exalted revelations of truth. This teaching, which is full of grandly expressive statements, constitutes the *Bhagavad-Gîtâ,* "Song of the Blessed," one of the high points both of Hindu ethics and of Hindu popular thought. The question whether the *Gîtâ* was originally an independent composition, or whether it was part of the epic from the first, is of interest to scholars alone.

The one hundred thousand verses (mostly couplets of thirty-two syllables) of which the *Mahâ-Bhârata* is composed are supplemented in a vast compilation called the *Harivamsa,* or "Genealogy of Hari" (i.e. Vishnu), a collection of myths and legends more or less closely associated with Vishnuism.

The Râmâyana

The other Epic, the *Râmâyana,* or "Saga of Râma," is markedly shorter (twenty-four thousand couplets) and more unified in its construction; its style, which is less archaic, points toward

[3] Renou, *The Nature of Hinduism,* chap. iii.

the courtly poetry that future periods were to bring to birth. But the story itself, like that of the *Mahâ-Bhârata,* is set in a mythical past, earlier, indeed, than that of the war of the Bhâratas. The poem is attributed to Vâlmîki, who probably gathered together the scattered material of oral tradition and combined it into a semi-learned collection.

The story that forms the opening section of the poem is crowded with episodes; it concerns the childhood and youth of the hero Râma, son of King Ayodhyâ (the modern Oudh), and his marriage to Sîtâ, daughter of the king of the Videhas, whose hand he obtained by an exploit like Arjuna's: the bending of a magical bow. But when the time comes for Râma to succeed his father on the throne he is driven out as a result of plots among the queens; he is forced to go into exile with Sîtâ and his brother Lakshmana. After various episodes in which Râma fights against demonic brigands, the Râkshasas, their chief, the demon Râvana, king of the distant island of Lankâ, resolves on revenge. He takes advantage of the brothers' absence to abduct Sîtâ, carry her off in his airy chariot and shut her up in his palace.

Râma concludes an alliance with the monkey-people, whose king is that much-loved figure of Indian myth and story, Hanumant. Crossing the ocean in a single fantastic bound, Hanumant manages to visit Sîtâ and encourage and console her. Râma then attacks Râvana's wondrous capital, having first led his armies across a bridge of rocks and trees. The demon army comes out in a body and is eventually put to flight; Râvana is killed by Râma, who liberates Sîtâ and returns in triumph to Ayodhyâ. Painful scenes follow: fearing that Sîtâ has not remained chaste during her captivity in the demon's palace, Râma repudiates her. She tries to throw herself into the flames, but the god of fire spares her and bears witness to her innocence. The last book gives a different version: Râma has the queen led into the forest to be abandoned. She gives birth to twins in the hermit's dwelling where she has been given refuge. Not till much later does Râma encounter his children; stricken with remorse, he tries to take Sîtâ away, but she utters an invocation to the earth, which opens to receive her.

The historical memories (allusions to an early Aryan colonization in southern India) are more credible in this Epic than in the other. But its general material is nonetheless legendary; probably, indeed, wholly mythical. The characters are somewhat conventional figures, with the foreground occupied by Sîtâ, the embodiment of purity, and Râma, the hero who is devoted to the Law even though his devotion sometimes compels him to behave inhumanely. Râma's divinization is dealt with in a few episodes of late date that may have been interpolations in the completed work.

Both epics have had considerable influence on the Indian literatures, not only in Sanskrit but in some of the other languages as well. The old stories have been rewritten over and over again, abridged, transformed into lyric or dramatic poems, and so on. In the case of the Râmâyana, indeed, we note the existence of a whole folklore with which Valmîki had nothing to do, and the diffusion of which was especially copious in Indochina and Indonesia. The Sanskrit version (which is extant in several recensions) is merely one of the branches of this folklore, a branch that has been tidied up and stylized.

The Purânas and the Tantras

The Epic is continued, after a fashion, in the enormously extensive literature of the *Purânas*. This is a literature without dates; it may have covered the whole of the first millennium of the Christian era. In addition to the major texts, the "Great *Purânas*," numbers of minor or "sub-*Purânas*," were produced: separate hymns, "glorifications" (of holy places), and other treatises inspired by a variety of subjects. The word *purâna* means "ancient," and the genre is already mentioned in the Vedic texts;

but as always, the written versions are of a later date, with the result that the language is usually a popular or semi-popular Sanskrit, not quite free from irregularities but containing none of the archaisms preserved in the Epic. The *Purânas* are definitely religious works, since they are dedicated to deities and supposedly propagated by them, and also since the strongest and most definite of the purposes running through them is the exposition of sacred legends and the description of religious practices, pilgrimages and so on; some of them were compiled to meet the needs of a particular sect. A number of them are (or were) of considerable length. But, though their general character is religious, the subject matter is historical or pseudo-historical: it consists, broadly, of an intermittent narration of the history of the world from time immemorial, tracing the cyclic periods that have elapsed from then until the advent of modern royal houses (some parts of whose histories are described in the form of prophesies). Finally, side by side with religious teachings, there are completely secular chapters on such matters as music, poetics, medicine, grammar and so on. All in all, the *Purânas* are really encyclopedias. The best known are the "*Purâna* of Vishnu," which is part of the relatively ancient stratum in the *Purânas* and gives a condensed summary of the mythology of Vishnuism; and the "*Purâna* of the adepts of the Blessed One" (*Bhâgavata-Purâna*), that is to say, of Krishna, which, in contrast to the other, ranks among the later productions (ninth century?) and is the most interesting of all the *Purânas* by reason of its elevated thought and superior style.

Other, similar collections have sometimes been classified as a group under the general name of *Tantras,* or "Books." More exactly, a distinction can be drawn between the *Tantras* properly so called, which are simply *Purânas* serving the needs of the special aspect of Hinduism known eponymously as Tântrism;[4]

---

[4] Renou, *The Nature of Hinduism,* chaps. iv and v.

the *Samhitâs*, or "Collections," in which are assembled the fundamental data of Vishnuism, for the use of the Vishnuite sects; and the *Âgamas*, or "Traditions," which perform the same service for Shivaism. Like the *Purânas*, these treatises contain cosmogony, hymnology and ritual; philosophical speculation plays a large part in them and sometimes assumes fantastic forms, These series, like the foregoing, cannot be dated; all we know is that important *Tantras* were compiled as late as the beginning of modern times, and that the earliest may have been produced, possibly under the stimulus of a form of Tântrism influenced by Buddhism, about the seventh or eighth century.

2 / BELLES-LETTRES

General: "Classical" Sanskrit

As early as the Vedic period, the learned language of the ancient hymns, which teems with images, provided favorable conditions for the development of lyric poetry. But there are no indications that Sanskrit was put to secular use in that period. Not until the second century B.C. do we observe, in the quotations provided by the grammarian Patañjali, the existence of lyrical strophes. And in fact the earliest complete works known to us, which are still more recent (first or second century A.D.), are Buddhist in design: it was Buddhism, perhaps imitating Brâhmanic models since lost, that first gave shape to poetry of the "classical" (kâvya) type. On the other hand, there must have existed a fairly early lyric poetry in Middle Indian, a fact that likewise presupposes the existence of Sanskrit prototypes. In this context as in many others, Sanskrit figures as a latecomer, either because the ancient works were lost or because the old theory of a "renaissance of Brâhmanism," as propounded by Max Müller, should be retained.

It is true that the requisite external conditions for creating a tradition of court poetry hardly arose before the time of the Guptas (beginning of the fourth century): these kings, the first in whom indigenous extraction was combined with allegiance to Hinduism, and who were in addition the masters of a huge empire and had an inborn love of magnificence, supported a number of poets, patronized their works, spurred them on to compete with one another, encouraged literary circles and discussions, and fostered literature as they did the other arts. The major lyrical tradition of India probably has its roots in this period, therefore, even if a few scattered inscriptions in Sanskrit, as early as the second century, contain expressions and verbal images that coincide with some of those to be found in literature.

Vedic Sanskrit, as it appears in the hymns of the *Rig-Veda*, gradually shed its linguistic archaisms and other vestiges of an earlier age, acquired simplicity and precision in its morphology and syntax, and became what is known as "classical Sanskrit," stabilized for all time by the grammarian Pânini. It is true that in the higher forms of literature, in texts that are the result of careful artistic elaboration, new complications arise, this time relating not to grammar but to style. The word order, in poetry at least, is arbitrary; the sentence is lengthened and heavily burdened with dependent phrases, relative and other subordinate clauses, with descriptive matter and incidental stories. Composite nouns, which have hitherto been kept within moderate limits, now proliferate so wildly as to produce, in certain works in learned prose, endless strings of verbal elements put together without any inflexional connection—an astonishing transformation in a language so rich in terminations and in grammatical capacities generally! Metaphors and comparisons increase and multiply; words with a double meaning are favored and are sometimes used in such combinations as to create whole sentences that can be understood on two levels simultaneously.

The vocabulary is enriched with a mass of new words, and certain archaic terms re-emerge from disuse with additional meanings attached to them. In short, a whole rhetorical convention is built up; different authors avail themselves of it in different degrees, but the later the period the wider its influence becomes. Some writers, however, and some genres, remain untouched by this verbal sophistication—whose nature is indicated by the very word "Sanskrit," *samskrita,* "(language) equipped with all the refinements (of grammar and style)."

It is obvious that, in the circumstances, Sanskrit was drifting away from the status of a spoken language. We do not really know just when it ceased to be colloquial. The most ancient inscriptions, those of the emperor Asoka (third century B.C.), are not in Sanskrit; no doubt the language was already the preserve of an elite and was used only in schools and among Brâhmans and literati. This state of affairs persisted for a long time; it is not certain that the extraordinary expansion of Sanskrit literature, starting in the fourth century, involved any real revival of Sanskrit as a spoken language. All the same, although Sanskrit was never truly colloquial except in some unfathomably remote period, it has also never really been a dead language; even today there are many people in different parts of India who can speak it, often with astonishing mastery. Many more still, even in the humbler levels of society, understand it.

In inscriptions, and in Buddhist and Jain literature (which were originally closed to it), Sanskrit steadily regained lost ground. Not until the appearance of the "modern" languages in the thirteenth or fourteenth century did it encounter any serious rival. Even in southern India, where from a much earlier date it had to meet the competition of the Dravidian languages, Sanskrit retained a powerful hold, even more powerful than in the north.

Kâlidâsə

The first great name in that stream of Sanskrit literature which is of Brâhmanic inspiration is that of Kâlidâsa. Forerunners are mentioned, but their names no longer possess any meaning for us (with the possible exception of Bhâsa). No certain date can be fixed for Kâlidâsa; he is generally held to have lived at the court of Chandragupta II (375-414), at Ujjayinî (the modern Ujein, in the Avanti region), where he was probably born. Chandragupta II was called Vikramâditya, "the Sun of Valor," and it is in fact to the reign of a certain Vikramâditya (who, however, is stated to have belonged to a more remote past) that tradition assigns the life of the poet, who was one of the "nine jewels" of the imperial court. There are various legends about Kâlidâsa's life; one of them has it that he died in Ceylon, under Kumâradâsa; others were occasioned by his very name, which means "slave of (the goddess) Kâlî."

As in the case of other great men, a large number of works have been attributed to Kâlidâsa. Of these, all that are certainly his are three plays that we shall examine below and three poems of the kind known as "great poems" *(mahâkâvya)*: minor epics of learned composition that can be described fairly exactly as lyrical epics. There is no such certainty about the authorship of another poem, which, in spite of some passages of unequal quality, is not unworthy of the master and might be a work of his youth. This is the *Ritusamhâra*, the "Round of the Seasons," a graceful description, loaded with erotic touches, of the six seasons that are supposed to make up the Indian year. If the work really does belong to Kâlidâsa's period, it is a brilliant first handling of a theme already current in Vedic times and destined to survive for a long time in all the Indian literatures: a description of nature in the different seasons, and of the various amusements and kinds of work proper to each, all within a factitious framework and, on some pretext or other, made part of a longer composition.

One of the three authentic poems is the *Meghadûta,* or "Cloud Messenger": a kind of elegy, serious in tone and composed with much subtlety. The story is that of a spirit or genius (Yaksha) who has been sent into exile in a distant province and compelled to leave his wife behind in his native country, to the north of the Himalayas. The Yaksha commands a passing cloud to take her a message of love and fidelity; he describes in advance the places over which the cloud will have to pass—cities, rivers, forests—on its way to the cherished place where his loved one is enduring her sadness. The poem is a masterpiece of delicate feeling, a perfect success in a type of literary art that, despite its learned and accomplished form, remains nevertheless simple, direct and moving. The "Cloud Messenger" touched off a long series of imitations, some in Sanskrit and some in other Indian languages. Many of these were composed in Malabar, where the local setting afforded a convenient pretext for various geographical and even religious variations on the original theme.

The *Raghuvamsha,* or "Lineage of Raghu," is a poetically idealized chronicle of the legendary dynasts who claim the Sun as their first ancestor. The most celebrated of these is the hero-prince Râma, whose dramatic story provides the core of the poem and is a condensation of the essential material of the *Râmâyana.* The work is uneven, but gorgeous descriptions and exciting episodes provide plenty of brilliant pages in this apparently unfinished epic of nineteen cantos; every effort was made to avoid monotony and barrenness of style. Included in the poem are a Round of the Seasons, a description of the Deserted City, the graceful pictures of the wives of Ayodhyâ gathering in haste to watch the procession of the princes, and the famous episode in which a young ascetic, going to the stream to fill a pitcher for his aged parents, is killed by an arrow intended for someone else.

The *Kumârasambhava,* or "Birth of Kumâra," a poem in eight cantos (to which a sequel was added by an overingenious imitator), despite its title does not describe the birth of Shiva's son, but the events preceding it: the story of the ascetic practices to which Shiva devotes himself in the Himalayas, and of how the divine maiden Pârvatî, who has fallen in love with him, succeeds in winning his love by devoting herself before his eyes to practices equally severe. There is the well-known scene in which the wrathful Shiva makes use of his "third eye" to burn up the god of love; there is also the picture of the wedding of the divine pair, a description set in that ambiguous key, half religious and half erotic, that is further developed and exploited in subsequent literature.

The poems of Kâlidâsa represent the peak of stylistic perfection in Sanskrit, a unique balance between the awkwardness or rough simplicity of early times and the preciosity that later overwhelms literary expression. Kâlidâsa is the faithful upholder of the Brâhmanic ideal; he exalts both the virtues of the *kshatriya,* the "nobleman," and those of the Brâhman. He is also aware of the lives of humble folk; setting aside convention, he succeeds without effort in speaking with a movingly human voice.

Major Lyric Poetry After Kâlidâsa

After Kâlidâsa, the "great poem" was much in favor. Traditionally, six of these poems (among them the three by Kâlidâsa) are regarded as models; but there are other that deserve to be ranked very high, at least if the postulates of the genre be admitted. The conditions of this were the narrow choice of subject matter and the artificial style and vocabulary—all the more exacting because of the passionate desire of most of the authors concerned to seek out new heights of finesse and new formal difficulties, in order to outdo their predecessors.

As in the *Raghuvamsha,* and more particularly in the *Kumà-*

rasambhava, the themes are borrowed from the vast repertory of the Epic or of the *Purânas.* The most notable works are the following:

The *Kirâtâjunîya,* or "Combat of Shiva (disguised as a *kirâta,* a mountain huntsman) and Arjuna," composed by Bhâravi, most likely in the sixth century: the story of the quarrel between the epic hero Arjuna and the god disguised as a hunter, both claiming the same prey. The quarrel degenerates into actual combat, the vicissitudes of which are ever more tremendous and which ends when Shiva is satisfied by the courage shown by his opponent. He reveals his identity, forgives Arjuna and showers him with favors.

The *Shishupâlavadha,* "Murder of Shishupâla," by Mâgha (eighth century, in all likelihood), relates a similar episode, drawn, as in the foregoing, from the *Mahâ-Bhârata;* but the inspiration is connected this time with the worship of Krishna, not Shiva. Prince Shishupâla has challenged the god Krishna; a prodigious fight ensues, in the course of which the god cuts off his insolent adversary's head with his discus. Even more so than Bhâravi, whom he has visibly sought to imitate, Mâgha deploys all the resources of a consummate technique: there are sets of stanzas with a double meaning, others that are arranged so as to make geometrical patterns, and so forth; the descriptions are overwhelmingly magnificent, and as in many similar *kâvyas,* the climax dwindles beside them; the great aim is to accumulate as big and impressive an effect as possible by means of description, and by mythological and philosophical allusions.

Poems of the same species have gone on being composed down to the present time—even Lives of Gandhi have been written in this style. An example that demands mention on account of its singularity (which is far from being unique) is a relatively early epic (possibly of the sixth century), the *Bhatti-Kâvya,* or "Poem of Bhatti" (= Bhartrihari?), which deals with the legend of Râma and at the same time, strophe by strophe and in the correct order, illustrates all the principal rules of grammar and poetics. A work of greater literary value is the *Naishadhacarita,* or "Story of Nala," by Shriharsha (twelfth century), which unfolds in twenty-two cantos the opening stages of the epic of Nala and Damayanti; or again, in the same period, the *Shrikanthacarita,* or "Story of Shrikantha" (= Shiva), by Mankha, in which the story of the demon Tripura's defeat by the god Shiva is drawn out into twenty-five cantos.

"Great poems" whose subject matter is historical show exactly the same methods of composition as the foregoing examples. The only difference is that the hero is a contemporary dynastic ruler, whose deeds it is the poet's business to extol in the same high-flown style as is employed for heroes or gods. There are few outstanding works in this enormous category, which increased and multiplied as petty principalities became more numerous; its heyday was the Râjput period, but it existed in all periods. Panegyrical inscriptions, which are often very long, can be regarded as an annex to this category. They are to be found from the period of the Guptas on; with more or less of *brio* in different cases, they borrow the phraseology of the poems.

One of these historical poems stands out from the rest: the *Râjataranginî* ("River of Kings") by Kalhana (twelfth century), a chronicle of the princes of Kashmir from mythical times down to Kalhana's own day. The style is simple and firm, and social description provides a felicitous contrast with the tale of battles and palace revolutions. The author's preoccupations are those of a moralist and social historian; moreover the degree of factual accuracy in his work is on the whole much higher than in most other poems of the same kind. Nowhere in Sanskrit literature, for that matter, is there to be found a historical work in the sense in which we understand that term.

In our own age, the poets who have distinguished themselves in the *kâvya* include Narayana Shastri, of Tanjore (1860-

1911), C. Ramashastri, of Madras, and C. Venkataramanayya, of Mysore; there have been many others, among them a woman, Kshamabai Roa of Bombay, whose work is simpler and more straightforward.

The Short Lyric

There is an abundance of shorter poems. Some are single short odes; others are arranged as longer units, which the poets are particularly fond of extending into "centuries," and which are either purely lyrical or else lyrical with a didactic bias. Two kinds of inspiration are manifest in this poetry, the sensual and the devout, and each to some extent merges into the other. Isolated stanzas, and groups of stanzas, were collected, from the eleventh century on, or perhaps earlier, into anthologies arranged in sections according to subject matter; these preserve the memory of many otherwise forgotten poets.

In the field of religious lyricism, there are not only innumerable hymns of more or less scholarly composition—some of which are attributed to Shankara himself and others to Kâlidâsa or to Ashvaghosha—but also, all through the Middle Ages, poems of a more popular stamp, whose orientation is in some cases that of Vishnuism or Krishnaism, in others, Shivaism or shaktism. The glorification of *bhakti*—a kind of emotional pietism that, at a certain point in time, arises to refresh and invigorate religious feeling[1]—inspired a large number of works, some of which were appropriated by the literature of one sect or another. But none of them attained such success as the *Gîtagovinda,* the "Singing Shepherd" (literally the "Sung Shepherd"), by Jayadeva, a Bengali poet of the twelfth century. Its language is far from being as correct as that of the scholarly lyrics, but the story (the love of Râdhâ the shepherdess and the young rustic god Krishna) is told with consummate art. As in the *Song of*

[1] Louis Renou, *The Nature of Hinduism* (New York: Walker and Company, 1962), chap. iv.

Songs, it is possible for the reader not to know (or to pretend not to know) whether the theme is sexual (as everything about the poem, if one takes it literally, seems to indicate) or whether it should all be transposed into religious terms. This naïve pastoral is presented somewhat in the manner of a libretto, the words appearing as a series of melodies that end with recurrent refrains.

Lyricism in a more direct and familiar key is represented by the poetry of Amaru, a mysterious character who cannot be identified but who may have lived in the seventh century. Each of his hundred or so stanzas contains an independent picture, describing in miniature the joys, fears, pains and reconciliations of lovers. His vivid, vigorous language enhances the value of these little scenes, which he delights to round off by the addition of some piquant touch. Mention must also be made of the "Fifty Stanzas of the Thief," by Bilhana (eleventh–twelfth century), in which the poet evokes the amorous delights he tasted in the arms of a young princess.

Other works, without differing much in form from those already mentioned, are written with the more practical aim of imparting a moral teaching or even a political one. An example is the "Centuries" of Bhartrihari (probably written between 600 and 700 A. D.), a collection of three hundred stanzas treating of love, worldly wisdom and renunciation. In this instance also, the main interest lies in the descriptions, in the realism of the detail, and in the general tone, which is emotional without being extravagant. But the basic and all-pervading intention is didactic; it even dominates the last section of the triptych, whose purpose is to show that all attachments and desires are vanity of vanities and that the one thing needful is to free oneself from passion and to pursue spiritual happiness. This work is one of the great creations of the peak of the Middle Ages in India; the fame of the "Centuries" is attested by the variety of recensions in which it has survived, and by the number of manuscripts.

It must not be thought that the Sanskrit lyric evolved only within the limits of an artificial convention. There exist collections of an entirely different kind—social satire, descriptions of the half-world of the courtesans and the underworld of the thieves, portrayals of hypocrites of all sorts. There are, for example, the richly scabrous "Lessons of a Procuress," by Kshemendra, a prolific writer of the eleventh century; and the same poet's "Flowering of the Arts," a depiction of the various vices. To Dâmodaragupta (eighth century) we owe a poem of the same kind, "Instructions for Courtesans."

In addition, the classical age, which began about the same time as the Christian era, produced an incredible profusion of gnomic verses. Some of these are independent compositions, others occur in the course of prose works on the most diverse subjects. Their authors apply themselves to expressing, in a more or less personal and surprising way, their own views on private conduct and social behavior, and on the consequences of vice or negligence or of virtue unintelligently exercised; at times the note they strike is skeptical or even irreligious. Many a miniature masterpiece, in which the conciseness of Sanskrit has worked wonders, lies buried in this vast poetic rubble.

The Indian Tale; The Panchatantra

The origins of Indian storytelling go back to the Veda, with its references to the fables and imaginative stories typical of any folklore. Naturally the written stories drew very largely on the immemorial riches of Asiatic tales. There was a time when scholars held India to have been the birthplace from which every story had proceeded; today we are ready to admit, even if stories from different parts of the world show close similarities, that they originated independently, at different times and in different places. However, the fact remains that ancient India, from the mass of anonymous oral tales, preserved materials for written work that were immediately and perfectly transmissible, so that the genre spread and prospered far beyond India herself. There is a scholarly prose; there was also a simple popular style or a simplified form of the learned style; stories of this kind were more numerous and appropriate to several kinds of public. The attitude expressed is religious and sometimes biased (very slightly) toward Brâhmanism, or, more frequently, toward Buddhism or Jainism. In some cases it is reasonable to infer that the Sanskrit text is the translation of a work originally composed in "Middle Indian."

The fable as a literary category, already in evidence here and there in the *Mahâ-Bhârata,* took shape in an immensely popular collection, the *Panchatantra,* or "Five Books." The recensions in which we possess it show divergences, and attempts have been made to reconstruct the original. We do not know when or by whom these recensions, which come from widely separated parts of India, were made; one of them, which is far from being the earliest, the *Hitopadesa,* or "Profitable Instruction," attributed to one Nârâyana, emphasizes by its very title the intention of these tales. They were to instruct by entertaining; they were parables to teach a young prince the value of prudent conduct and enlightened counsel. They illustrate, in popular form, the Purânic treatises on policy and practical wisdom.

The stories in the *Panchatantra* are usually in prose, with an inlay of gnomic verses. The leading characters are usually animals, but these often move freely among human beings; and the jackal, the lion's minister, plays the part that in the West is given to the fox. Most of the storytelling is quite perfect in its limpidity and simplicity.

These collections made their way to the West incognito, as it were, through translations based on one or another of the Sanskrit originals. The oldest of these translations is that in Pahlavi, from the sixth century. This translation was the hub from which radiated versions in various European and Near Eastern languages, ancient and modern, while translations from Sanskrit or Middle Indian recensions spread into eastern and northern Asia. A total of over two hundred texts in some sixty different languages has been identified, the largest diffusion on record for any book except the Bible. Many great works, from the *Reineke Fuchs* and the *Fabliaux* to La Fontaine and the stories of Grimm and Andersen, imply more or less massive (though unwitting) borrowings from the Sanskrit source. On the other hand, philological reasons make doubtful any connection between the *Panchatantra* and the fables written in the tradition of Aesop.

The Brihat-Kathâ Cycle

As to stories in the real sense of the word, the earliest collection that has come down to us is the *Brihat-Kathâ*, the "Great Story," an enormous group of tales attributed to Gunâdhya, a semi-legendary figure. The original (written, it would seem, in an aberrant dialect derived from Sanskrit) is lost; it can be hypothetically dated as belonging to the opening centuries of the Christian era. Secondary versions of it have survived, the most famous being the *Kathâsaritsâgara*, the "Ocean from the Stream of Tales," by Somadeva, a Kashmiri author of the eleventh century. Written in an elegant, supple Sanskrit, it is a series of three hundred and fifty versified tales, which are so many digressions from a central story that the reader gradually forgets. The hero is a prince from the country of the Vatsas who sets out to look for his wife, who has been spirited away by an unknown aggressor. He finds her at the end of the story after a succession of adventures, some dovetailed into each other. In short, it is a kind of *Râmâyana* set in the key of light entertainment. Its realistic scenes and its depiction of manners and customs—despite the aura of legend and fairy tale surrounding them—make this romanesque story very valuable. It is one of our chief sources of information on what life was like in medieval India.

Among the best of the stories told by Somadeva are the "Twenty-five Tales of the Vampire," which were no doubt originally an independent group. The structure is particularly striking: to please a yogin, the king agrees to go by night to a cemetery and remove the corpse of a man hanging from a tree. This corpse is inhabited by a "vampire" *(vetâla)*, who entertains the king by telling him stories. In each story there is a question to which the king must give a suitable reply. At the end the Vetâla, satisfied by these replies, endows him with mastery over magical forces.

This framework makes one think of the "Thousand and One Nights"—in which several stories give grounds for inferring that here again there was a borrowing from some Indian source. The same device of accessory narratives is found in other celebrated works in Sanskrit: for example, in the "Thirty-two Tales of the Throne" (the *Vikramacarita,* the "Story of Vikrama"), of uncertain date, in which the hero is the fabulous prince Vikramâditya. Of greater literary value are the "Seventy Stories of the Parrot" *(Shukasaptati);* like so many other collections, this also became famous outside India—starting in this instance in Iran. The stories are invented every evening by a parrot in order to divert a young wife whose husband is absent and who is thinking of taking a lover. So interested is she in what is going to happen next that she keeps deferring her intention. The irony of it all is that most of the stories are about adultery, and show how women's cleverness enables them to triumph in situations of mortal danger.

The Novel

Novels in Sanskrit are few, and hardly deserve the name. They are really expanded tales, written in the same sophisticated

and often precious style as the scholarly lyrics. The earliest—
and the most acceptable by reason of its narrative excellence
and comparatively simple style, which make it the masterpiece
of Sanskrit literary prose—is the one attributed to Dandin,
doubtless from the sixth or seventh century. This is the *Dashaku-
mâracarita,* the "Story of the Ten Young Men," a typical example
of what may be called the "loose-leaf" composition. Each of
these youths, who are the sons of ministers or kings, relates the
adventures he has had during a "conquest of the dominions of
the East," a comic imitation of the grandiose royal expeditions
described in the Epic. Despite their deliberately complicated
episodes, these stories maintain interest throughout; picaresque
and often scandalous themes are heightened by passages of
subtle moralizing and by numerous descriptions of manners and
customs.

Little need be said of the irksome preciosity of *Vâsavadattâ* (the title is the heroine's name), by Subandhu (seventh
or eighth century), a novel much prized in India. Possibly about
the same period there arise the first of the *campûs,* romances
with epical subjects written in passages of verse and prose al-
ternately; this technical form has continued to our own day, the
outstanding example of it being that by Somadevasùri.

The development of the "novel" after Dandin is really confined to the two works of Bâna, the court poet of the emperor
Harsha, who was the last purely "Hindu" monarch before the
Moslem invasions. The *Harshacarita,* or "Story of Harsha,"
which describes the life of his royal patron, is valuable less for
its historical accuracy, though that is beyond reproach, than
from the extraordinary plenitude of its descriptions—life at
court, great ceremonies, military expeditions, even village or
jungle scenes, on occasion. Its literary craftsmanship is the
height of Sanskrit style, with virtuosity enough to delight the
connoisseur, but discouraging for anyone who, without ade-
quate preparation, tries to enter this universe of riddles, of composite words interlacing to form endless sentences.

Bâna wrote another work in the same style, though with perceptibly simpler passages here and there: *Kâdambarî* (the heroine's name), a languid tale full of fantastic and marvelous elements. It is esteemed as the acme of Indian literary art. It recounts (backward, from the end to the beginning of each, as the *kathâ* technique demands) the adventures, during their successive lives, of two pairs of lovers who are cruelly parted by fate; the story defies analysis. Like the other, this romance owes its merit to its descriptions of towns, landscapes and characters. It is bathed in an atmosphere of tenderness and peace that has a subtle charm of its own.

As for the problem of a relationship—which is historically not impossible—between the Sanskrit novel and the Alexandrian novel, no certain answer can be given. The idea has now been given up, though no one denies the existence of parallels between the two, possibly reflecting a common substratum differently utilized.

The Drama; Kâlidâsa

The drama, too, has its origins in the Veda, at least if we regard as prefigurations of drama the dialogue hymns in the *Rig-Veda* (which have been variously interpreted), and if we include the quasi-dramatic scenes that are part of Vedic ritual. So in this direction the drama seems to have religious connections; in any case these are undeniable, since they are confirmed by the many common elements to be observed in historical times between the theatre on the one hand, and religious legend and the practices of worship on the other. In the Middle Ages the processions, or *yatrâs,* were—notably in Bengal—accompanied by dramatic performances; everywhere we see these two activities side by side. On the other hand, the theatre also had its roots in popular life: in mime, village drama, comic sketches and, possibly, puppet plays and shadow plays. The survival of these rudimentary forms of theatre can be seen even in Sanskrit artistic drama; it is this drama that we shall now study.

Scholars had long suspected the existence of Sanskrit drama earlier than Kâlidâsa, but it was not until 1910 and the years immediately following that "archaic" drama was discovered. In Central Asia some allegorical fragments were found whose tendency was Buddhistic, and which were attributed to Ashvaghosha; also, and more especially in southern India, thirteen comedies were discovered, and immediately attributed to Bhâsa, a predecessor of Kâlidâsa. The latter attribution was soon contested and can no longer be regarded as definitive; some scholars even hesitate to believe that the comedies are earlier than Kâlidâsa, but this seems excessively prudent. These plays are short and rather elementary in style and construction; written in simple language, they treat subjects drawn from the Epic or the *Brihat-Kathâ*. The best of them is *Svapnavâsavadattâ*, "Vâsavadattâ the Dreamer," a romantic comedy that shows a genuine instinct for the stage.

To Kâlidâsa we owe three dramatic works, of different degrees of interest. "Agnimitra and Mâlavikâ" is the prototype of the harem comedies that were subsequently produced in considerable numbers. A princess is living incognito at the king's court; the king falls in love with her, but the queen surprises them together, and things would turn out badly but for a *coup de théâtre* in which it is revealed that the girl is of royal origin herself; the queen can therefore accept her as a co-wife without any loss of dignity.

The second play, *Vikramorvashî,* "Urvashî (won by) Heroism," is the touching story, told frequently from Vedic times on, of an Apsaras (a kind of nymph) who has fallen in love with a mortal. It is told as a dramatized fairy story, and some of the scenes show impressive scope and imaginative power.

But the masterpiece, not only of Kâlidâsa but of Indian dramatic art as a whole, is *Shakuntala,* or, to give it its full title,

"Shakuntala (won) by the Sign of Recognition." The subject is taken from the Epic, but freely adapted. King Dushyanta has strayed into the depths of the forest in the course of a hunting expedition. He reaches a hermitage where he meets the girl Shakuntala, the daughter of an Apsaras. They fall in love and consummate their love in secret. However, the king returns to his capital, promising to send for his lover later, and leaving his ring as a token of his promise.

But Shakuntala, lost in her dream of happiness, has omitted to salute an irascible ascetic, who now casts a curse upon her. The king seems to have forgotten her and she tries in vain to make him recognize her; but she has lost the ring that alone would enable her to revive his remembrance of her. Shakuntala's mother carries her up to heaven. Some time afterward the ring is found by a fisherman. The king recovers his memory and sets out in search of the young woman, but in vain. Much later, however, he meets a boy whom he questions and discovers to be his son, born of his union with Shakuntala, who is now at last restored to him.

Building on thoroughly Indian foundations, the poet has created a work of lasting beauty; its delicate emotions, its fascinating descriptions of nature, and its subtle alternation of moving and amusing scenes make up its character. The style throughout has the sober elegance that is the mark of a master hand.

In the plays of Kâlidâsa, Sanskrit drama has all its characteristic features, also present in part in Ashvaghosha and the pseudo-Bhâsa. The dialogue is written partly in straightforward prose, partly in highly wrought stanzas that are usually descriptive and are in some cases intended to be sung. The "noble" characters (but not the women) speak Sanskrit; the others speak Prâkrit, and in theory at least, different kinds of Prâkrit are allotted to different castes and functions. As time went on, some, but not many, plays were written entirely in

Sanskrit or entirely in Prâkrit. For the rest, the theatre was subject to rules as minute and as precisely formulated as those of the poetic doctrine governing the "great lyric."

The Drama After Kâlidâsa

There is a charming comedy, the *Mriccakatikâ* ("The Terra-cotta Chariot"), which may be contemporary with Kâlidâsa but about whose author "Shûdraka the King," we know nothing. The plot is rather unusual: it is the story of the fondness between a high-souled courtesan, Vâsavadatta, and a merchant, Chârudatta, who has ruined himself by his religious benefactions. The love of these two is crossed by the malevolence shown toward the merchant by the king's brother-in-law, who is in love with the courtesan. He attacks her one day when she is on her way to see Chârudatta, leaves her for dead, and accuses the young man of the murder. Through a series of fatal coincidences Chârudatta is convicted and is about to be executed, when the victim enters in the nick of time to save him; and a palace revolution delivers the country from the tyrannical brother-in-law. Despite being—inevitably—stylized, the piece is very much alive; indeed it is the furthest inclined toward realism of all the Sanskrit plays, and one of the most thorough in its involvement with society and custom. In somewhat the same vein as the "Chariot" is a political play whose action is managed fairly neatly, "Rakshasa-of-the-seal" by Vishâkhadatta or Vishâkhadeva (fifth century?), which makes a stage character of the famous Chânakya, the unscrupulous minister of King Chandragupta, the founder of the Maurya dynasty.

In the seventh century—at least if their attribution to King Harsha is maintained—we have three elegantly written, agreeably constructed plays: two harem comedies, of a kind not far removed from comic opera, the better of them being *Ratnâvalî* (the heroine's name); and a third, which is both amorous and edifying and shows Buddhist influence, the *Nâgânanda,* or "Felicity of the Nâgas."

A dramatist whose merits are held to rival those of Kâlidâsa is Bhavabhûti. In all probability he flourished in the early part of the eighth century, but his name is hardly known to us save by the attribution to him of three important works. Two of them consist of a manipulation of material from the *Râmâyana,* the more noteworthy being the "End of the Story of Râma" (*Uttara-râmacarita*); the third, "Mâdhava and Malatî," is a love intrigue heightened by violent, tragic scenes (tantric rites and human sacrifice). Bhavabhûti has neither the delicate touch of Kâlidâsa nor his moderation; he possesses power, brilliance and a vocabulary that, though sometimes rhetorical, is rich and expressive. His plays are a little on the static side, but that is a fault easily forgiven in India, and found in most subsequent Indian plays.

Here we cannot even mention the titles of the most important of these plays; there are so many, and it is so difficult to distinguish from the general mass those that depart, however slightly, from a theatrical convention that becomes more and more rigid. The established genres are faithfully kept up, and the plot is always either borrowed from the ancient literature or taken ready-made from the comedy of manner.

However, there are a few pieces that deviate from the beaten track, such as the "Play of Hanumant," a kind of recitative entirely in verse that tells the popular story of the monkey who was Râma's ally. Some scholars have maintained that this play and a few others show the influence of the shadow theatre, which is to be found all over Southeast Asia.

There are plays inspired by sectarian devotion, in which the characters are sometimes allegorical figures. And finally, just as there are historical epics, so, too, there are historical dramas, in which the principal character is a dynast or some other notable personage, whose merits are celebrated in a resoundingly rhetorical style.

So much for the elevated or "noble" theatre. The theorists also describe a great variety of minor genres, for the existence of which we have little or no direct evidence; two *vîthîs* have recently been discovered. Two of these genres deserve mention on account of their singularity: the "farces," in which a plot about lovers is used as a vehicle for social and religious satire, often extremely free; and the "monologues," in which a witty *bon vivant* tells of the amorous and other adventures that have befallen him during the day, and exchanges remarks with interlocutors who do not appear on the stage.

In our own time, plays are still written in Sanskrit—some of them traditional, others making a break with tradition, or purporting to do so. Among the best may be cited those of Professor V. Raghavan of Madras, Mahalinga Shastri (also of Madras), and Narayana (already mentioned).

3 / THE LITERATURES OF INDIAN TECHNIQUES

Philosophy

A considerable proportion of Sanskrit literature is philosophical. In addition to what may be called the technical literature of philosophy, which we shall discuss in greater detail, there is a more popular tradition already active in the Vedic hymns, which is continued in the *Upanishads* (which continued to be produced from the end of the Vedic period to the sixteenth century), and supplies part of the impulse behind the *Purânas* and *Tantras*. Quantities of poetic works in the Middle Ages, and of religious treatises composed under the aegis of one or another of the various sects, are penetrated through and through with *Vedânta* or *Sânkhya;* and philosophical disquisitions abound in grammar, poetics, medicine and other disciplines. But the essence of the Brâhmanic doctrines is contained in what is known as the *darshanas.* The word means, properly, "views," that is to say, the different aspects assumed by philosophical thought, particularly in relation to the ultimate goal of all philosophy, the achievement of salvation.

The *darshanas* are six in number, and embrace all the "orthodox" methods; however, some authors say there are more, including even the Skeptics or Materialists, whose literature is almost completely lost. The *darshanas* appeared in the early centuries of the Christian era, in the form of *Sutrâs*, "aphorisms": these aphorisms immediately became the subject of commentaries, oral at first, later written down, which were sometimes developed into semi-independent works or, as more frequently happened, gave rise to further commentaries; and so the process has gone on, even into contemporary times.

The *darshanas* are:

a) *Mîmâmsâ* (more strictly, *Pûrva-Mîmâmsâ*, "first Mîmâmsâ"). The word means "reflection (on the act)"; the system is commonly regarded as having been founded by Jaimini, and there were some two thousand seven hundred *sûtras*. It was originally a sort of dialectic, a kind of reasoning about the most essential act of all, namely the ritual act as defined in the Vedic texts. *Mîmâmsâ* sets forth the rules of interpretation that allow the intentions of the earliest theorists of Vedic worship to be exactly realized, and any ambiguities or apparent contradictions to be resolved. Little by little, *Mîmâmsâ* developed a kind of logic susceptible of being applied to other domains as well, for instance, in juridical discussion, where it was much used. Later the system evolved into a theory of knowledge, a metaphysics, a theory of language; it turned toward soteriology, but never lost its original connections with ritual. Its great names are those of Shabarasvâmin (probably fifth century), the earliest author of a written commentary on the *Sûtras;* Prabhâkara (seventh century?); and, above all, Kumârila (eighth century, a native of southern India), who wrote treatises of primary importance. The literature, which is extensive, has never ceased being added to.

b) *Vedânta* lies closer to our own preoccupations and is of greater general interest. The name means "Purpose of the

Veda." Another name is *Uttara-Mîmâmsâ,* "Second *Mîmâmsâ*", *Vedânta* being regarded as a continuation of the speculations of the foregoing system. The *Sûtras* of *Vedânta* are attributed to Bâdarâyana. *Vedânta* develops the philosophical theses of the Vedic *Upanishads* in the ontological and monistic direction that is the leading characteristic of these ancient texts. It is also based on the *Bhagavad-Gîtâ,* which, with the *Sûtras* and *Upanishads,* forms the "triple point of departure" of *Vedânta.* But in fact, although the whole of *Vedânta* starts with the same premises, no system has shown a greater number of divergences. Shankara, who was the first of the great commentators on the *Vedânta Sûtras* (or, as they are also called, the *Brahma-Sûtras*) and the greatest name in Indian philosophy, kept the doctrine strictly within the framework of an inviolate non-dualism *(advaita),* that is to say, a conception of being in which the *brahman* (neuter) is the only transcendent reality and the world is only an attribute of *brahman.* Shankara, a Nambudiri Brâhman from Travancore, pretty certainly lived in the eighth and ninth centuries (though this date has been disputed); he is thought to have created ten monastic orders and to have preached all over India. A considerable body of written work is attributed to him, in which poems are interspersed with commentaries on the main *Upanishads,* on the *Gîtâ,* and especially (this being his masterwork) on the *Brahma-sûtras.* The literary output of the Shankaryan school has been immense; two of the great names are those of Mâdhava in the fourteenth century and Madhusùdana in the sixteenth, and philosophical and mystical movements in present-day India still lay claim, rightly or wrongly, to the *advaita* doctrines.

But the other forms of *Vedânta,* which came to birth from the tenth century on, or perhaps earlier, mostly depart from Shankara's uncompromising metaphysic; they introduce values that are specifically religious, under the influence of *bhakti,* which, from the ninth or tenth century on, began to impregnate nearly all philosophical speculation other than the Shankaryan; from then on *Vedânta* developed in association with one or another of the great sects, either Shaiva or, more commonly, Vaishnava.[1] The earliest of these "sectarian" movements is that created, or at least fostered and extended, by Râmânuja (eleventh or twelfth century; born near Madras), the upholder of a "qualified non-dualism" in which the *Brahmasûtras* provide the foundation for the idea of a personal, qualitative *brahman,* and deliverance is conceived as consisting in participation in the divine. The other leaders of this school are Yâmunâchârya (earlier than Râmânuja), and Vedântadeshika (also known as Venkateshvara) (thirteenth-fourteenth century).

In the thirteenth century a "dualistic" movement was inaugurated by Madhva, whereas Nimbârka (probably his contemporary) sought to reconcile dualism and non-dualism. In the sixteenth century, Vallabha (born near Benares of a Telugu family) claimed to return to pure non-dualism, but his doctrine was in fact quite different from that of Shankara; it included a concept of divine grace already developed by Râmânuja. The literature of these various schools is extensive.

The Shaiva sects[2] frequently produced more widely deviant forms of *Vedânta,* incorporating themes from *Sânkhya* (see below); thus the Kashmiri schools of the Trika, "Triad," whose most important commentator was Abhinavagupta (tenth-eleventh century), started from the ninth century on to develop a type of *Vedânta* at once realistic and idealistic; its counterpart in the south was the *Shaivasiddhânta* ("Shaiva doctrine") movement, in which the fundamental texts are not in Sanskrit (or at least have perished in their Sanskrit versions) but in Tamil.

With the advent of Chaitanya, *Vedânta* shows a definitely

[1] Shaiva means connected with the worship of Shiva; Vaishnava with that of Vishnu.—Tr.
[2] Louis Renou, *The Nature of Hinduism* (New York: Walker and Company, 1962), chap. vi.

more popular tendency; but the adepts of Chaitanyism built up a theology that was as learned as any other and that, like most of these sectarian branches of speculation, devoted much care to the elaboration of cosmogonic conceptions; this tendency produced the literature of the Gosvâmins (fifteenth century and later), which provided Bengali Vishnuism with its "canon."

c) *Sânkhya,* the "(System) founded on enumeration," is a dualistic philosophy that takes as its absolute principles *prakriti* (nature or matter) and, confronting this, the plurality of souls, or *purushas.* It accounts for the totality of phenomena, both physical and physical, in terms of the successive interaction of twenty-five factors. *Sânkhya* was originally a mechanistic and atheistic doctrine and remained so for a long time; but it eventually took a theistic turn and became one of the methods of access to deliverance. The foundation text, which is attributed to Kapila, has been lost; the Sûtras that are considered to represent it are of late date, having been either written in the fourteenth century (perhaps) or else rewritten about that time; where ancient times are concerned their place is taken by the collection of "Mnemonic Verses" of Ishvarakrishna, which was translated into Chinese as early as the sixth century. This collection was the subject of commentaries and subsidiary commentaries, to the eve of modern times; one of the important names in this development is Vijñânabhiksu, in the sixteenth century. A number of works from the *Upanishads* to the Epic and the Tantras, are impregnated with *Sânkhya* doctrines.

d) In addition, it was *Sânkhya* that provided Yoga with a philosophical structure, and enabled it to rise to the status of a *darshana.* Properly speaking, *Yoga,* the "(method of) Union," is a method of attaining to superhuman powers and, at the highest level, to complete mystical mastery.[3] The doctrine of *Yoga,* which was set down by Patañjali in the customary form of "aphorisms," gave rise to a succession of commentaries, one of

[3] Ibid., chap iv.

the most important of which is that of Vedavyâsa (about the eighth century). Patañjali's treatise deals with *Râja Yoga*, the highest or "royal" form of the yogic discipline; lower forms were also evolved, such as *Hatha-Yoga*, or "*Yoga* of violence," the main object of which is the control of internal bodily processes. Having its origin in the Veda (for example, in Vedic passages dealing with pneumatology, ascetic "heat," and so on), and perhaps also in an earlier, shamanistic tradition, Yoga permeated the whole of tântrism, and its philosophical aspects provided a major theme of philosophical inspiration from the time of some of the *Upanishads* and the *Gîtâ* to modern times, when the position has been compromised and the word "yoga" has become a general term denoting any method of spiritual attainment.

e) Nyâya, or the "Rule," the basic text of which is thought to have been written by Gautama, is first and foremost a method of reasoning, a formal logic with rather different foundations from those of Aristotle's logic. A theory of knowledge was attached to it at an early stage; subsequently, in conformity with the tendencies reigning in all these disciplines, a theistic-type ontology was added. The literature, which is very extensive, consists in the first place of the series of long commentaries, each deriving from its predecessors (Vâtsyâyana, fifth century, ?; Uddyotakara, seventh century; Udayana, tenth century), which constitute the ancient school of *Nyâya*. The polemic of the Buddhist logicians, which develops and proliferates between the sixth and eleventh centuries, gives way from the twelfth century on (Gangesha or Gangeshvara) to a return to pure logic and Brâhmanic values; this is the "new school" or Navadvîpa school (after Nuddea in Bengal).

f) Lastly, *Vaisheshika,* the "(System) based on specification," defines categories (substances, qualities and so on) and erects a doctrine that is realistic (in the philosophical sense) and has atomistic tendencies. Its *Sûtras,* which are attributed to

Kanâda, have been made the subject of many commentaries, starting with that of Prashastapada (probably fifth century). A remarkable feature is the fusion of *Nyâya* and *Vaisheshika* in a single continuous exposition; such expositions are found in treatises that appear at intervals from the twelfth century on, perhaps earlier; these are simple and elementary for the most part.

Some texts give a summary description of the "six *darshanas*" and add other orthodox or heterodox "systems." Some writers commented on several *darshanas* simultaneously; an example is Vâcaspatimishra of Mithilâ (ninth century), who wrote on almost all of them; another is Appayadikshîta (Kânchi, sixteenth century), who became outstanding in several branches of *Vedânta*, both sectarian and non-sectarian.

Scientific and Other Techniques

From earliest times the Indians were concerned to give methodical expression to the doctrines and practical instructions related to the various disciplines that gradually took shape and emerged from the narrow field of religious usage, to which they were originally confined. Vast series of classifications were established, with definitions and a whole technical vocabulary that in most cases was precise and well thought out; in some instances the Indians had recourse to immediate experience and even experiment, but as a rule they preferred to speak of things in terms of convention and tradition. A religious origin is claimed for the earliest writings on phonetics, astronomy and geometry. In fact, in ancient times, every major technique was regarded as having been divinely revealed; every important text was regarded as the descendant of an earlier teaching whose ultimate source was a communication from one of the great gods. Brahman, and later Shiva, were the founders of the major literary disciplines; Ganesha was the patron.

Grammar and Lexicography

Vedic philosophical speculation often has a basis in grammar and presupposes a certain semantic or etymological knowledge. From early antiquity a pseudo-etymological exegesis of the *Rig-Veda* was developed, namely the *Nirukta* ("Interpretation") of Yâska. Other conceptions, which were evolved little by little and which concerned the symbolism of sound and the invisible powers of the spoken word, were combined with more positive views to create what has been termed a philosophy of grammar, the source from which the Mîmâmsists and the Tântrists were to draw when composing their speculations on language. The essential document in this field is the *Vâkyapadîya*, "(Treatise on) Expressions and Words," by Bhartrihari (seventh century?).

On the other hand, grammar properly so called was faithfully described—without philosophical speculation—by Pânini (fifth century B.C.?), whose work goes under the name of *Ashtâdhyâyî*, "The Eight Chapters." One of the oldest grammars in the world, this is also one of the most perfect. It is drawn up in the form of "aphorisms," about four thousand in all, which are barely comprehensible without the help of a commentary. Using conventional signs and a system of references and abbreviations, Pânini manages to give a complete picture of Sanskrit, even including topics from the Vedas, in less than thirty pages. This treatise possesses considerable historical importance; Sanskrit, which was still in a fluid condition as the period of the Vedic disciplines drew to a close, was definitively fixed by Pânini; it became the reliable, exact instrument that for centuries was to be the means of expression of an immense civilization.

There are numerous commentaries on Pânini; they have gone on appearing from time to time until the present day. The most important among them is the *Mahâ-Bhâshya*, the "Great

Commentary" of Patañjali (second century B.C.), which contains additional rules; some of these are borrowed from the *vârttikas,* that is to say, the "complements" put together by his predecessor *Kâtyâyana.* A popular gloss still current is the *Kâshikâvritti* (seventh century), the "Gloss of Benares."

From the early years of the Christian era and thereafter, other grammars, modeled on Pânini, make their appearance in distinct "schools"; at first among the Buddhists and Jains, later among the Brâhmans, among whom from the twelfth century on there also appear adaptations of Pânini for use in schools. Finally, it may be noted that most grammars of Prâkrit are written in Sanskrit; the oldest (though its date is not known) is that of Vararuchi.

Lexicography, like grammar, was founded in terms of the Vedic vocabulary. But the first important dictionary is that of Amarasimha (date uncertain), the *Amara-kosha* (from the abbreviated name of its author). In it the material is broadly arranged in semantic groups, with appendices on "homonyms" and parts of speech. It is a popular work, still learned by heart, and has given rise to more than fifty commentaries. It is followed by a long succession of dictionaries *(kosha),* some general, others specialized (prominent among the latter are dictionaries of botanical medicine); and the arrangement is sometimes by synonyms, sometimes by homonyms.

Finally, prosody, in which the basic text is the "Aphorisms on the (Vedic) Meters," by Pingala (of uncertain date), has been the subject of a number of treatises, several of which include Prâkrit prosody.

Poetics

A body of teaching on poetics, or perhaps we should rather say on rhetoric *(Alankâra-Shâstra,* "Instructions on the Ornaments of Style"), must have been closely modeled on the practice of the first literary texts, giving summary practical rules on qualities and defects, rhetorical figures, "styles" and "manners," and the expression of different emotions; then, as lyric poetry developed in volume and variety, poetics, on the rebound from its early dependence, seems to have taken the upper hand over the artist's work and to have imposed on it an ever-increasing degree of stylization. The earliest treatises to have been preserved, the *Kâvyâdarsha* ("Mirror of Poetry") by Dandin, and the *Kâvyâlankara* ("Adornment of Poetry") by Bhâmaha, may have been written in the seventh century. After this there is a long line of manuals and commentaries until the seventeenth century. The theories or *rasa* ("poetic savor")[4] and of *dhani* ("resonance") give the movements a speculative bias, especially in the work of Abhinavagupta (tenth-eleventh centuries). Abundant lyrical quotations accompany the rules and explanations.

If poetics is unlike many other disciplines in possessing no fundamental document, dramatic art does possess one: the *Nâtya-Shâstra* ("Doctrine of Dramatic Art"), attributed to Bharata. This substantial work (of undetermined date) is a sort of encyclopedia, dealing not only with the theatre properly so called, but also with all the arts connected with the stage, including poetry and music; the most important commentary on it is that of Abhinavagupta. In more recent periods there have been adaptations and imitations of the *Bhâratîya,* and there are also traces of independent dramatic treatises; finally there are works that combine dramatics and poetics, while others refer especially to the art of the dance, or mime, and so on.

Literature on music is very abundant, and can claim Vedic origin in the treatises based on the *Sâma-Veda.* We know, from long lists of authors' names, that music continually provided the

---

[4] See in A. K. Coomaraswamy, *The Dance of Shiva* (rev. ed.; New York: Farrar, Straus and Cudahy, 1957), "Hindu View of Art: Theory of Beauty," for an admirable exposition of the doctrine of *rasa.*—Tr.

subject matter for more or less detailed manuals, the oldest of which are unfortunately lost. The best known, such as the *Sangîtaratnâkara* ("Mine of the Jewels of Music"), by Shârngadeva (Kashmir, thirteenth century), must be based on much older material. Such treatises have continued to be written in our own day, and are grouped in various "schools."

Law

The literary origins of Law, the *Dharma-Shâstra* ("Teaching Concerning *Dharma*"), are in the "Aphorisms of *Dharma*," which date from the Vedic epoch; as might be expected, these aphorisms display the stamp of religious life, as indeed does the whole of the literature in question. Nevertheless the purpose of the great classical treatises on *dharma*, constituting what is known as the *Smriti*, is to set up an autonomous system of law, in which they often incorporate political and economic teachings and also, widening the scope still further, observations on the life of society. The best known and one of the oldest (dating perhaps from the dawn of the Christian era) is the one that evokes the mythical law-giver of all mankind, Manu: the "Laws of Manu," or, in an alternative and more accurate form of the title, the "Teaching Concerning *Dharma* According to the Mânava School" *(Mânava-Dharmashâstra,* or *Manu-Smriti).* This is a versified collection of juridical and social maxims set in a cosmogonic and eschatological framework; its poetic quality is perceptibly higher than that of other similar works. The *Laws of Manu* have inspired an abundance of commentaries and served as the model for innumerable other *Smritis.* Subsequently, from about 1000 A.D., various Digests were compiled in which the material is presented in a more systematic and technical fashion; for example, the famous *Mitâksharâ,* the "(Treatise) With Measured Syllables," by Vijñâneshvara (almost certainly of the twelfth century), which in most of India is still regarded as authoritative. It consists of a freely written commentary on an ancient *Smriti*, itself of very high repute, known as the *Smriti* of Yâjñavalkya. Special treatises were also composed, bearing on such subjects as adoption and the laws of inheritance. Moreover, information similar to that given in the *Smriti*, and at least equally ancient, is conveyed in lengthy passages of the *Mahâ-Bhârata*, in some of the *Purânas*, and also, for example, in that gigantic *summa*, the "Ideal Jewel of the Four Aims (of Human Life)," by Hemâdri (thirteenth century). Finally, Indian schools of thought on law, particularly Manu, expanded into Southeast Asia: inscriptions bear witness to their influence from the sixth century on.

Political and Social Economy

While the Smriti texts give scope to the study of economic and political norms, this discipline also has an independent literary domain of its own: the *Artha-Shâstra*, or "Doctrine of Prosperity," the fountainhead of which is a very important work, the *Artha-Shâstra* of Kautilya; the manuscript was discovered in 1910. The author is supposed to have been the same Kautilya (alias Chânakya or Vishnugupta) who was minister to Chandragupta the Maurya, which would place his work in the fourth century B.C. This dating does not hold good for the whole text; in the form in which we possess it, the compilation (for such it is) cannot be earlier than the third or fourth century A.D., but it contains much older material and seems to show traces of another work that was adapted and incorporated. However this may be, the *Kautilîya* constitutes a mine of information, much of it unique, on royal administration, internal and foreign policy, civil and penal law, and war. It is written in a difficult, concentrated prose (with stanzas of verse scattered here and there) in which it is possible that some earlier set of "aphorisms" lies embedded.

The works that come after the *Artha-Shâstra* are of much less importance; some are specialized studies of political policy *(nîti);* others, of various aspects of economic life. As elsewhere, there is no lack of simple, instructive maxims, the inclusion of which is a tradition going back to the *Mahâ-Bhârata.*

It is legitimate to connect with the *Artha-Shâstra* a group of studies that are more or less adumbrated in the *Kautilîya* but do not achieve their full development until a later period. The most important of these is the *Shilpa-Shâstra,* "Doctrine of the Arts": a succession of works devoted primarily to architecture and secondarily to town planning, the arrangement of furniture and so on in houses, and also to vehicles, machines, images of the deities, and various other subjects. The subject matter of the *Shilpa* is dealt with by many other works; some that are directly devoted to it also contain religious passages pointing out the "revealed" origin of the *Shilpa.* The classic work in this field is the *Mânasâra* ("The Essence of Construction"— if the title is authentic); its date and authorship are not certain.

Another branch of studies, related to the study of *Artha,* is the *Dhanur-Veda,* the "Veda of the Bow," under which are grouped the many books on war and the military arts. With the same branch we may associate the copious literature on the Horse and the Elephant; works on pearls and precious stones; on games and sports; and many others of which an exhaustive list cannot be given here. As in all branches of secular literature, the number of texts preserved (and often very poorly preserved) is small in comparison with the number lost or mutilated.

Erotic Science

The theory of "pleasure" *(kâma)* is enunciated in didactic works that, in addition to a description of sexual techniques, usually contain elements of eugenics and characterology, details of feminine dress and adornment, the home, the life of the lover and of courtesans, and even information on religious ritual. Both the lore as a whole, and the most famous and possibly the oldest exposition of it, are known as the *Kâma-Shâstra;* the exposition in question is more properly entitled *Kâma-Sûtras,* "Aphorisms on Pleasure" (for it is written in semi-aphoristic prose, with a short piece of verse to end each chapter); the author is Vâtsyâyana, who may have lived in the fourth century. After Vâtsyâyana there is a copious literature, much of it inspired by him; at times it borders on dramatic literature; it also touches on medicine and magic. A work of a slightly aberrant type is the "Book (of the Life) of the Lover," by Padmashrî (date unknown).

The Sciences

Scientific works in the proper sense are far from being as numerous, taken as a whole, as the preceding categories. Nevertheless the Indians left notable works in several fields, mainly written in Sanskrit.

Their achievements were particularly great in medicine. While the Vedic texts contain or imply certain medical doctrines and a certain amount of practical knowledge in medicine and the pharmacopoeia, we must look to the first centuries of the Christian era for the appearance of comprehensive technical manuals (and even these are not free of philosophical speculation): the two great *Samhitâs* ("Collections"), attributed respectively to Charaka and Sushruta. Charaka is reputed to have been the physician of Kanishka, which would give the second century as a possible date for him. The *Samhitâ* of Sushruta is more recent and is especially concerned with surgery. Another great name, coming somewhat later, is Vâgbhata (seventh century). Indian medicine, as represented by these works (as distinct from other, later types, those with Arabic or Buddhist influence, not to mention the paramedical elements in tântrism and Yoga), is known as the *Âyur-Veda*, the "Veda of Long Life," and claims the mythical Dhanvantari as its patron. It has points of resemblance to the treatises of Hippocrates, but this may be a matter of coincidence, for the *Âyur-Veda* is thoroughly Indian in its thought and its manner of expression, and implies moreover that in certain ways the Indian technique of medicine was more advanced than the Greek. The ancient treatises are either in verse or in a mixture of verse and prose; examples in a "Prakritized" Sanskrit have been discovered. A glance over the literature as a whole shows it to be rich and varied and to include not only general works but also specialized studies (on ophthalmology, for instance), medical dictionaries and so on; and medical works conceived in the most traditional spirit have continued to be written even in our own day. The *Âyur-Veda* has had much influence on non-Sanskrit Indian medicine and has penetrated into Central and Southeast Asia.

Alchemy derives from a different tradition, and its pharmacopoeia is mineral. But alchemistic research was scientific in character at first: it was a rudimentary chemistry, concerned with practical problems, a marginal activity connected both with medicine and with metallurgy. It was gradually invaded by speculative ideas and came to be regarded as an independent means to mystical attainment. Some of the alchemistic texts are attributed to Nâgârjuna; if this is so, they belong to the second century.

In astronomy, evidence of fairly advanced knowledge is found early, in the Vedic literature; this knowledge had been fostered by the need to establish the religious calendar correctly and also by the exigencies of certain of the Vedic rites. One of the contingent branches of Vedic lore was *Jyotisha*, "astronomy"; its main object of study was the zodiac of twenty-seven or twenty-eight "houses." It has sometimes been assumed, but entirely without proof, that the Indian doctrine of the zodiac was an importation from Mesopotamia or China. *Jyotisha* also included a computation of the "great year" and its fractions, which has some similarities with ancient Greek astronomy. Systematic manuals of astronomy make their appearance much later, beginning in the fourth century A.D. with the *Sûryasiddhânta*, or "Doctrine of the Sun," an anonymous work in five hundred verses. This is followed by treatises of a more technical nature, many of which contain elements of arithmetic and algebra; it seems that in this realm the Indians can claim the invention of the symbol for zero and the discovery of its positional value, the extraction of square and cube roots, the discovery of the number pi, and more besides.[5] The important authors are Âryabhata in the fifth or sixth century, Brahmagupta in the seventh, and Bhâskara in the twelfth. There are also some isolated mathematical manuals, such as the *Ganitasâra* ("Essence of Calculation") of Shrîdhara (eleventh century). The *Lîlâvatî* ("The Gracious One"), which is part of Bhâskara's compendium, presents mathematical problems in an entertaining, poetic way.

Indebtedness to Greek influence is confined to terminology. Borrowings occur more frequently in astrology, in works that sometimes mingle astrological information with astronomical. There are handbooks dealing with the astrology of natural phenomena, with the individual horoscope, with omens (the origins of the last-named branch lie in the "appendices" of the *Atharva-Veda*), and with every variety of divination. The best-known work is one that overflows the confines of astrology proper, the *Brihat-Samhitâ* ("Great Collection") of the astronomer Varâha-mihira (sixth century), a versified treatise containing a wealth of information on the most varied topics.

[5] The story of Indian achievements in early mathematics is interesting and impressive. It seems to have included the discovery of continued fractions, which were known as "pulverization"; a reference will be found in Sir Thomas Heath's edition of Diophantus (Oxford, 1910). For an Indian proof of the theorem of Pythagoras by dissection, see Hugo Steinhaus, *Mathematical Snapshots* (rev. ed.; New York: Oxford University Press, 1960).—Tr.

As for pure magic, a remarkable collection of magical prescriptions was devoted to it as early as Vedic times: the *Kaushika-Sûtra*, the work of one of the *Atharva* schools of thought. Further texts appear later, several of which are attributed to Nâgârjuna (who may or may not be identical with the Buddhist teacher of the same name; if he is, the works concerned are from the second century). These texts provide a link between the *Kaushika-Sûtra* and the various magical doctrines that crop up widely in the tântric texts, and that are imbued with speculative influence.

4 / BUDDHIST AND JAINIST LITERATURE

Buddhism

Sanskrit was not the principal medium of expression for the
Buddhist and Jain religions. Their determination to react
against Brâhmanism, and their desire to remain at a linguistic
level closer to that of the people, led them to abandon Sanskrit.
This was only a temporary change; Sanskrit rapidly made its
way back as the medium for writings of Buddhist and Jain
provenance, in the early centuries of the Christian era; a little
later it also regained its place as the language of inscriptions.
Moreover, one of the sects of primitive Buddhism or *Hînayâna*
(the "Minor Vehicle," according to the conventional rendering),
the Sarvâstivâdins, who flourished in Kashmir and later in
Mathurâ, had retained Sanskrit (though perhaps in a form con-
taminated by Middle Indian) as their canonical language; this
version has disappeared for the most part, though important
fragments have been discovered in modern times in Kashmir,
containing, in particular, "sermons" *(sûtras)* of the Buddha, and

passages from the "rule"; other fragments were discovered somewhat earlier at Turfan and other places in Central Asia.

Later on, an enormous Sanskrit literature arises, for which there is no parallel in Middle Indian. It was most frequently translated into Chinese and Tibetan, and the Indian original can now be reconstituted only by means of these foreign versions. The whole make up what is known as Northern Buddhism, the "Great Vehicle" *(Mâhayâna)*, in contrast to the Southern (Singhalese) tradition of the "Minor Vehicle," which remained faithful to Middle Indian.

There are, to begin with, narrative texts of the kind known as *avadâna*, which relate pious deeds (though it is not quite certain that "pious" is the correct translation); that is to say, they make use of impressive, attractive stories to illustrate the close connection between the deeds of a lifetime on earth and those of past or future existences. The earliest of these *avadânas* are part of the "Minor Vehicle"; an example is the collection known as the *Avadâna-Shataka* (the "Hundred *Avadânas*"), which may date from the second century. A similar but more remarkable collection is the *Divyâvadana* ("Celestial *Avadânas*"); this was the work of the Sarvâstivâda school and is imperfectly preserved in Sanskrit; it contains some of Buddhism's most moving stories. The *Jâtakamâlâ*, or "Garland of the Former Lives (of the Buddha)," in prose with verse here and there, by Aryadeva (fourth century?), is perceptibly more stylized.

Among the "sermons" *(sûtra)* of the "Great Vehicle," the first place must undoubtedly be accorded to the *Saddharma-puntarika*, the "Lotus of the Good Law," a relatively early text in verse and prose (a Chinese version of it was made before 316); it describes, rhetorically and with a lavish display of images and flourishes, the ideal of the *bodhisattva* (young Buddha during his spiritual apprenticeship), and glorifies the supreme Buddha; it stands in some sense as a counterpart to the *Bhagavad-Gîtâ*, and became immensely popular in every country where the expansion of Buddhism made itself felt.

A work of no less importance is the *Mahâsvastu*, the "Great Subject," in verse and prose, deriving from the Hînayâna school of the Mahâsânghikas. It narrates various events in the life of the Buddha in the form of a novel or fantasy, with edifying anecdotes thrown in. No less fantastic and of similar composition is the *Lalitavistara*, the "Particularized Account of the Games (of the Buddha)"; this, too, is a biography of the Master, full of miracles and legends. Both these works may belong to the third or fourth century; both are written in a hybrid Sanskrit; we do not know for certain whether this replaced a Middle Indian original or whether it represents an attempt, not quite carried through, to make Sanskrit conform to a Middle Indian pattern.

Two other important works are on a more didactic level: the *Bodhicharyâvatâra*, "Entry Into the Way of Life (Leading) to Illumination," and the *Shikshâchamuchchaya*, "Sum of Instruction," by Shântideva (seventh century); the second is doctrinal and written in a dry, unexpressive style, but the first is full of ardent faith and displays brilliant literary capacities. Didactic also, but rather low in the scale of artistic values, is the *Mahâyâna-Sûtrâlankâra* ("Ornament of the *Sûtras* of the Great Vehicle"), by Asanga (more probably the work of Maitreyanâtha, third century), which is written in "verses-for-memorizing" of the Yogâchara school; another didactic work is the *Lankâvatâra(-Sûtra)*, the "Revelation of Lankâ (Ceylon)," which was translated into Chinese in 443 and which sets forth the theses of the Vijñânavâdins. There is a whole series of *Sûtras*, many of them lengthy, describing the "perfections" of the *bodhisattva*, especially the "perfection of Wisdom": these are the *Prajñâ-Pâramitâs*, the oldest of which were translated into Chinese in the second century and after. They enjoyed a considerable vogue and were the subject of learned commentaries by the great masters of the *Mahâyâna* tradition: first by Nâgârjuna (traditionally supposed to have been a Brâhman born in southern India and converted to Buddhism, probably of the third century), and next by the brothers Asanga and Vasubandhu (third-fourth centuries), who were born in the extreme northwest. The Sanskrit form of these commentaries has been lost. To the same masters we owe other works of which the originals were not lost; thus, in the case of Nâgârjuna, we have the *Mâdhyamikârikâs*, "Verses of the School of Mâdhyamika," a school of which he was the founder and which develops the thesis of the universal void *(shûnyavâda);* his principal successor was Chandrakîrti (sixth century). The school of the Vijñânavâdins (upholding the thesis that "All is consciousness") is represented by a work that is in fact valid for all the other schools, too: the *Abhidharmakosha* ("Treasure of the *Abidharma"),* by Vasubandhu, the original of which was recently rediscovered.

A later work, more poetic in character, is the *Suvarnaprâbhasa,* "The Golden Splendor," an ethical and philosophical composition with an admixture of legends and panegyrics of the gods; the first extant Chinese translation belongs to the fifth century. The *Gandavyûha,* which represents the tendencies of the Avatamsaka school, became widely known in China, as did most of the treatises already mentioned and many others that there is no room to mention here.

In logic, the works contributed by Buddhist thinkers come soon after the first Brâhmanic commentaries on *Nyâya.* Dignâga, the first of the Buddhist logicians (probably earlier than the fifth century), has survived almost exclusively in translations; but we possess the Sanskrit original of the major work of Dharmakîrti, the *Nyâyabindu,* with the commentary on it written by Dharmottara in the eighth century. Dharmakîrti was born in the seventh century at Tirumalla, and defended Dignâga against the attacks of Uddyotakara. There is a succession of further texts until the twelfth century, at which time Brâhmanic logic regains the upper hand and keeps it.

There is, finally, a Buddhist form of tântrism, known as *Vajrayâna,* the "Diamond Vessel," which flourished from about the seventh century and produced books of ritual, mythological dithyrambs and "means of magical realization" *(sâdhanas);* a typical work of this kind is the *Mañjushrî-Mûlakalpa,* which is supposed to be of the Avatamsaka school and is specially concerned to expound the virtues of magico-mystical "formulae" for repetition. Texts of this sort reached Tibet and China from the eighth century on and, in India itself, exerted an influence on the Hindu *tantras.*

The Sanskrit in which they are written is more or less uncouth. Moreover, most of the Buddhist texts (even if we overlook those couched in "hybrid" diction) show morphological and syntactical peculiarities related to those of Middle Indian. This is what is called "Buddhist Sanskrit"; it differs as widely from normal Sanskrit as does "Jain Sanskrit," the latter type used in works of Jain inspiration, which we shall discuss in a moment.

However, there are a few works in which the Buddhist writers did their best to emulate Brâhmanic models in point of elevated diction and stylistic beauty. The poems attributed to Ashvagosha must be placed in the first rank. He was a contemporary and protégé of King Kanishka, which means that he was probably of the second century; he is thought to have been born in Ayodhyâ (the modern Oudh), but we know nothing definite about his history. Religious tradition credits him with a large number of major and minor works, of which only a very few were really written by him. The latter include two "lyrical epics," exactly in the style of the *mahâkâvya*—which one might well believe to have inspired them but for the surprising fact that these two epics are earlier than any of the known Brâhmanic examples of the *mahâkâvya.* The same author's *Buddhacharita* ("History of the Buddha"), only part of which has survived in Sanskrit, displays a constant care for order and artistry, and its edifying aims never lead the author into the fantasies and excesses so common in works about Buddha. The same poetic qualities are shown in the *Saundarananda,* "Nanda the Comely," Buddha's half-brother, whom Buddha converted and who was ordained a monk. It is true that, compared with Kâlidâsa and his successors, the effect made by Ashvaghosha is somewhat turbid; he is something of a primitive, but the beauty of the feelings that inspire his works, and the brilliance of his images, more than make up for anything rough and unfinished in the expression. Among the other works attributed to Ashvaghosha are some dramatic fragments that we have briefly mentioned already, and (though here the attribution is uncertain) a *Sûtrâlankâra* ("Adorning of Sermons") or *Kalpanâmanditikâ* ("Harmony of Poetic Arrangement"—if the Sanskrit title is correct), a collection of stories in prose and verse, in an ornate style.

Finally, let us mention in passing that the Buddhists were fairly active in various technical disciplines, such as medicine and grammar Chandragomin (sixth or seventh century, Bengal) particularly distinguished himself in the latter.

Jainism

The preaching of Jains, which, like that of the Buddhists, began in the sixth century B.C., was not delivered in Sanskrit. But that language becomes more and more firmly established in the so-called post-canonical works, during the early centuries of the Christian age. The use of Sanskrit enriches, first, Jainism's enormous religious and parareligious output: dogmatics, ritual, ethics, edifying legends; next, every kind of imaginative work —romances, dramas, lyrical tales and epics; and finally, treatises on grammar, astronomy, mathematics and other subjects—the forerunners of all these treatises being already present in the canonical literature of Jainism. We cannot give the facts in much detail here. We may start by noting, where narrative literature is concerned, that the Jains surpassed in quantity, if not in quality, the very plentiful output of the rest of India. It must be admitted that this was achieved by their more adroit use of the common stock, and even of specifically Brâhmanic legends; for instance, they handled over and over again, from the period of the Canon on, the stories of Râma and Krishna, interweaving them with their own legends, whose principal features were the mythical lives of the twenty-four Tîrtham-kâras ("Prophets," the forerunners of the Mahâvîra) and their contemporaries, the Chakravartins ("Universal Sovereigns"). Hagiographical distortion is even more in evidence than among the Buddhists. The epoch of the great philosophical discussions (controversy with the upholders of *Mîmâmsâ* and those of classical *Nyâya*) covers the seventh and eighth centuries. Among the more prominent writers we must at least mention Haribhadra (eighth century), who is reputed to have written over 1,400 works; Siddharsi (early tenth century), the author of a famous allegorical romance; Amitagati (late tenth century), whose two didactic poems were widely known; and finally, and most important, Hemachandra (Gujrât, 1089-1172), poet, scholar and one of the most prolific and varied authors in medieval India. A special place of honor must be reserved for one of the earliest Sanskrit treatises, the *Tattvârthâdhigama-Sûtra* ("Manual for Understanding the Nature of Things"), by Umâsvâti (second century?), a summary of Jain dogma that adheres closely to the Canon.

There are several lyrical works comparable in quality to those of the main Indian tradition. The Jains proved themselves better than the Buddhists at assimilating the rhetorical rules, and the virtuosity, of the great classics. The model work in this genre is the *Yashastilaka* ("Brow Adornment of Fame"), by

Somadevasûri (tenth century), an epic of the *campû* type that abounds with information on Jain doctrine and also on Hindu sects. Naturally, commentaries on the Sacred Books occupy a large place in this literature, the growth of which has never ceased.

Conclusions

Sanskrit literature developed without a break from Vedic times on—that is to say, for 3,500 years at least—despite the temporary eclipse produced for some six or seven centuries by a vigorous literary growth in Middle Indian. No literature in the world has had so long a life; and the mass of extant works (only a small quantity, compared with what there must have been once) is one of the richest and most varied literary organisms that has ever existed. It spread all over India, with areas of special strength in Kashmir and indeed the whole of the northwest; in Bengal; and finally in Dravidian territory. It has had a lasting influence on the cultures of the Central and Eastern Asiatic peoples.

Its leading characteristic is fidelity to tradition. It is this that causes, in almost every domain, the same type of text to be produced again and again; it also causes a real or fictitious adherence to a "foundation text," and gives the character of a "commentary" to much of the scholarly prose. At the same time, this fidelity makes writers and readers comparatively indifferent to contemporary fact (even in supposedly historical romances and poems); new material is slow to be reflected in Sanskrit literature.

Even today, literary and scholarly composition in Sanskrit is far from negligible; several schools give instruction in the language; and periodicals are published. The Indian Constitution exists in a Sanskrit version that is intended to be its authoritative form, and some Indians even go so far as to look forward to the restoration of the "language of the gods" as the official language. That is utopian. But the elite of India have the task of preserving the vitality of Sanskrit and its literature; of in fact maintaining Sanskrit in the place that Latin occupied in the West at the time of the Renaissance. Not only is it impossible to interpret the modern Indian languages and the works written in them, save by reference to Sanskrit (and this applies even to a considerable part of the Dravidian languages and literatures); Sanskrit is, in addition, the foremost instrument of an intellectual and artistic tradition in which the culture of an age-old people is concentrated, and which every educated Indian should willingly and unreservedly support.

Part Two / The Middle Indian Literatures

5 / THE MIDDLE INDIAN LITERATURES

General

The dialects of which "Middle Indian" is composed are deriva-
tives of Sanskrit; in some respects, indeed, they are closer to
Vedic than to "classical Sanskrit. They preserve the essential
features of the ancient tongue, but they are at an advanced
stage of development by the time they come before us; phonetic
structure has suffered change and attrition, morphology has
been dislocated and simplified; vocabulary has changed in some
degree, partly through the intrusion of colloquial or regional
words, partly because these dialects have been modified and
adapted to the purpose of propagating heterodox religions,
namely Buddhism and Jainism. For the Buddhist and Jain
Canons, which are considered to reflect faithfully the teaching
of the Founders, the Buddha and the Jina (Mahâvîra), are in
fact drawn up in Middle Indian (with a partial exception in the
case of the Buddhist Canon). We possess proof that the Buddha
spoke one of these dialects and that his preaching helped to
propagate it. Nonetheless, the first dated evidence we have is

not literary but (as is usually the case in India) epigraphical. The evidence consists of rock and pillar inscriptions that, about 250 to 230 B.C., were made on the borders of his empire by command of the emperor Asoka the Maurya, after his decision to renounce violence and become the protector of the Buddhist ideal. These are approximately the most ancient Indian inscriptions. They are written in different Middle Indian dialects, evidently corresponding to their respective localities; taken as a whole, they are a little more archaic than the literary documents that come after them. Middle Indian thereafter held its place as the language of epigraphy until the second century A.D. at least, before giving way to Sanskrit, as official Hinduism progressively took the lead from Buddhism and Jainism.

Pâli

Pâli (which properly means "text"; "sacred text," as opposed to "commentary") is the name for the form taken by Middle Indian as the language of the Buddhist Scriptures, at least in their most commonly used version which serves as a vulgate in the southern traditions (the school of the Theravâdins). The geographical origin of Pâli has long been disputed: the tendency today is to prefer western India as its birthplace, but there is no decisive evidence that this is correct. Pâli is a relatively archaic idiom, simple and fairly uniform, stylistically not far removed from the language of the *Upanishads* and characterized (as that language is, but much more so) by repeated statements and the reiteration of set formulae; a feature that "Buddhist Sanskrit," imitating Pâli, also adopted. The Canon is supposed to have been created in Ceylon; tradition says this took place a little before the Christian era. The commentaries were compiled from the fifth century on by Buddhaghose (of the province of Magadha) and his adepts, but the earliest manuscripts we possess date from the tenth century, when the grammarians set about the systematic description of the language. By that time there existed, in addition to the Canon and the commentaries written directly upon it, a copious post-canonical literature, all of which was created in Ceylon. It is concentrated on the Sacred Books but embarks on the most varied subjects: edifying stories in verse and prose in the spirit of the "Minor Vehicle," historical chronicles (such as those inaugurated by the *Dîpavamsa* and the *Mahâvamsa* in the fifth century or thereabouts), imaginative works and works of erudition. The Burmese schools of thought take part from the fifteenth century on. In our own day Pâli is still a living, spoken language, not only in Ceylon itself but in all parts of Southeast Asia, to which Singhalese Buddhism spread its influence; the language has left its stamp on regional idioms, and has also undergone a perceptible internal evolution as a result of adapting itself to the new needs imposed on it.

The Pâli Canon is arranged in "Three Baskets" *(Tipitaka),* that is to say, in three sets of texts relating to the monastic rule (*Vinaya*), the Master's collected Sermons (*Sutta*, from Sanskrit *sûtra)* and lastly, dogma *(Abhidhamma).* The *Vinaya* illustrates the accepted repertory of anecdotes that show, as the *Brâhmanas* do, the reasons for every item of religious practice; the oldest part of the *Vinaya* is the *Pâtimokka*, which contains the form of service for public confession. The *Sutta(pitaka)* is mainly composed of four "Collections" *(Nikâya),* partly arranged in accordance with the length of the pieces they contain, as is the case with the Vedic hymns. It contains all the discourses and dialogues of the Buddha, with a few of those of his first disciples; some passages are in verse. A fifth collection was added, made up of short pieces and including the famous *Dhammapada*, a sequence of 423 verses describing in colloquial and often entertaining fashion the popular ethic of early Buddhism. The *Dhammapada* is one of the successes of Indian gnomic art. Another well-known collection, the *Sutta-Nipâta,* is written in a more formal style and contains fifty-five poems, one long and the others short, some of them narrative but most of them didactic, cast in the form of dialogues or ballads, with many touches of highly effective writing. This is one of the earliest parts of the Canon. In the *Thera-Gâthâs,* and especially the *Therî-Gâthâs,* that is to say, the "lays" supposed to have been composed by notable monks *(thera)* or nuns *(therî),* there are likewise pieces to be found that show a high pitch of art. These "lays" are a kind of elegy, semi-profane in type. As for the large collection of Sermons, all we shall mention here is the impressive account of the last days of the Buddha's earthly life, the *Mahâ-Parinibbâna(-Sutta),* the "Great Discourse on the Perfect Nirvâna (of the Buddha)."

The fifth series in the *Sutta-Pitaka* includes the enormous collection of the *Jatâkas* ("Nativities"), which consists of some five hundred edifying stories about episodes in the previous lives of the Buddha. But in fact the only canonical parts are the stanzas in archaic diction that accompany these stories; the prose was added later. The collection includes tales, fables (in which animals frequently change their shape), anecdotes and ballads drawn from various sources and connected with the Buddha by a conventional device: the initial stanza recalls that the Buddha, on such and such an occasion, told his followers the story of an episode from one of his previous lives. At the end of the story he identifies the characters evoked in it with those of his entourage at the time of telling. These little tales abound in delicate, graceful and, in many instances, moving touches; the Buddhist ethic frequently endows the details with great charm but does not detract from the imaginative quality of the tale or obscure the fine shades of feeling depicted. The *Jatâkas,* moreover, are a mine of information about a society that is no doubt partially unreal but that nonetheless has its roots deep in the very soil of Indian life. From India the stories made their way to various peoples of both East and West, being considerably travestied in the process. The date at which the *Jatâkas* were given their definitive form is not easy to establish; some of them were already in existence in the second or third century of our era, as is shown by the bas-reliefs at Bharhut and Sânchi, which faithfully reproduce scenes from them in stone.

The last great series in the *Tipitaka* is a sort of "complement to the *dhamma* (Buddhist law)," whence its name, *Abhidhamma*. It contains seven treatises dealing with various realms in dogmatics and philosophy.

The Prâkrits

The other Middle Indian dialects can all be grouped together under the generic designation Prâkrit. This denotes a "basic" language, a language that is "bare, denuded of ornament," in contrast to Sanskrit. There is in fact a whole series of Prâkrits, variously used and attested, corresponding, at least partially, the regional variations based on a kind of *koinë*. The strictness of grammatical conservation varies from one of these idioms to another; some of them are deviant. On the literary plane we find them being used both for Jain religious purposes and, concurrently with Sanskrit, in numerous works of a Brâhmanic character, and in purely secular ones, too.

The secular use of the Prâkrits first becomes manifest in the drama: as we have seen, Sanskrit drama sometimes includes passages in Prâkrit written to fit the rank or social function of the characters on stage. At a late period there are even a few plays written in Prâkrit throughout, such as the curious harem comedy *Karpûramañjarî* (the title is the heroine's name), by Râjashekhara (tenth century). The dialects concerned are *shaurasenî*, used in familiar dialogue, and *mâhârâshtrî*, chiefly used in stanzas intended for singing; there are others, which are used less. But *mâhârâshtrî* is used in a much wider field than the theatre alone: it is found in fairly early narrative or lyric poems, such as the *Setubandhu*, "The Building of the Bridge" (also known as *Râvanavadha*, "The Murder of Râvana"), a lyrical epic in scholarly style of unknown authorship (Kâlidâsa's name has been suggested), treating of some of the central episodes in the *Râmâyana*. Similar in composition is the *Gaudavaha* ("Murder of (Prince) Gauda"), by Vâkpatirâja (eighth century), an apparently unfinished pseudo-historical epic, which clothes a panegyric of King Yashovarman in a succession of legendary or descriptive scenes.

Of higher value than these too-learned compositions is the anthology attributed to King Hâla and known under various titles, all of which amount to "Collection of the Seven Hundred Strophes." These verses seem to have been collected by some amateur or other (the attribution to Hâla, which dates the work rather dubiously in the second century, cannot be considered reliable), with the aim of preserving a kind of poem that had passed out of fashion, and that was based on the imitation of folk songs. Most of them are pastorals: subtle, delicate miniatures, enlivened by a grain of malice or embellished with an elegantly presented image or maxim; many of these little scenes hinge on some matter of love or love-making, to which the rustic setting gives a rather ambiguous quality. The rhythms of the language are well managed and the vocabulary is rich and precise. There are several different recensions of this work, which poses difficult problems for the philologist.

The Jain Prâkrits, as they are called, are those in which the canonical and paracanonical texts of the Jains are written. "Semi-Magadhî" (from the name of the province of Magadha) *(ardhamâgadhî)* is regarded as having been the language of the founder of the Jain community, the Mahâvîra, who lived at the same time and in much the same locality as the Buddha (sixth century B.C., in Bihar). However, one of the two great sects of ancient times, the Digambaras, who do not recognize the Scriptures of the rival sect, the Svetâmbaras, adhere to a scriptural canon written in another dialect, related to *shaurasenî.*

The Svetâmbara tradition, the only one really known, has as its Canon a vast group of treatises embracing ritual and the rule of life, dogma and philosophy, legendary biographies and religious stories, and also a certain amount of secular instruction. The texts fall into categories similar to those of the Buddhists, but their content is often more mixed and their style often obscure and inflated. The most ancient portions are those grouped as *Angas*, "Members" (as the Veda, too, was divided into *Angas),* numbering twelve in all, and *Uvangas*, "Secondary Members," likewise twelve in number. After this come single texts or short series of texts, of which we must mention at least the *Uttarajjhayana(-Sutta)*, which contains some parables of great value and some beautiful ascetic poems.

The most important parts of the Canon may have been given their definitive form in the two or three centuries following the death of the Founder; some sections of it are certainly later. The language, deliberately archaic in some passages, is on the whole more developed than Pâli.

Finally, the extra-canonical literature, whose origins go back to the first centuries of our era, is written (except when Sanskrit was used) in a dialect similar to *mârâhârâshtrî*, known as Jain *mârâhârâshtrî*. In both languages this literature contains a mass of books of various kinds—dogmatic, narrative, lyrical and dramatic, and, in particular, religious tales or legendary biographies. An early epic poem (traditionally assigned to the first century) is the Paumachariya, or "History of Padma," by Vimalasûri, an adaptation of the legend of Râma in one hundred and eighteen cantos. The important period lasts until the eighth century, but production has gone on down to our own day, especially as regards interminable criticisms, commentaries and subsidiary commentaries on the Scriptures. The works of *digambara* provenance, of which there are fewer, are written in a slightly different idiom, for which the name "Jain *shaurasenî"* has been suggested. The *Pavayanasâra,* "The Essence of Discourse," by Kundakunda (soon after the birth of Christ), is the authoritative work in the philosophical field. The *Vasudeva-hindi* ("Wanderings of Vasudeva"), by Sanghadâsa (?; earlier than the sixth century) is merely adapted from the *Brihat-Kathâ.*

The Buddhists for their part hardly used the Prâkrits at all; or else nothing of their work in those dialects has come down to us. One of the schools of the Minor Vehicle, the Sthaviras, was reputed to have borrowed *paishâsî* (a northwestern dialect that seems to have been the medium of the original *Brihat-Kathâ)* as its canonical language. Another school, the Mahâsânghikas, must have used *mârâhârâshtrî;* a third, the Sammitîyas, is reputed to have used *apabhramsha,* which should be mentioned in completing this chapter.

Apabhramsha is a Prâkrit that is both more aberrant and more developed than the others; the very name means "(idiom that has) fallen (away from the norm)." It is used to describe certain works of Jain influence, mostly from between the tenth and twelfth centuries. Some of these are important, and, moreover, *apabhramsha* is freely used with common Prakrit or with Sanskrit; the narrative or lyrico-narrative element predominates in it, and the style and prosody are often highly cultivated, and at least as elaborate as those of the great classical lyric. There are reasons for believing that the writings in question come from western India, and that the origin of the dialect (which, however, is varied and cannot have come from one locality only) lies much further back in the past than they do. The most famous author of poems of this kind is Pushpadanta (tenth century), to whom we owe, in particular, an "Adornment of the Virtues of the Sixty-three Great Men (of Jain Antiquity)," or (more simply) a "Great *Purâna,*" an immense work of legendary biography divided into one hundred and two books. Mention may also be made of a work that is not Jain, the *Sandeshârâsaka,* a poem of the "message" type that was written in the twelfth century by a Moslem author known by the Hindu form of his name, Abdala Rahamâna.

A special type of *apabhramsa* was maintained in Bengal; it is the medium of the mystical stanzas of Saraha and those of Kânha (between the eighth and eleventh centuries), which are known as the *Dohâkoshas*, or "Collections in the *Dohâ* Meter." These poems give expression in popular terms—which are, however, completely hermetic—to certain themes of Buddhist tântrism.

Part Three / The Dravidian Literatures

6 / THE DRAVIDIAN LITERATURES

General

The Dravidian languages are a massive group covering the greater part of the Deccan. There are also sporadic Dravidian "islands" in northern India, the vestiges of an expansion that at one time carried this linguistic family as far afield as present-day Baluchistan.

Outside India there are no languages related to Dravidian, though various hypotheses have been put forward to prove the contrary. Dravidian is characterized by prominent features both phonetic (a tendency for internal consonants to be voiced and initial consonants voiceless) and morphological (development in the use of suffixes and in agglutinative processes, the expression of cases by means of postpositions, negative conjugation, and so on); and finally by a classification of vocabulary into superior nouns and inferior nouns (also called high-caste nouns and nouns of no caste). Certain features are common to Dravidian and modern Indo-Aryan. Word borrowings from the Indo-Aryan languages, notably Sanskrit, have been numerous at all levels of Dravidian culture; they have naturally been more marked in literary usage that depends on one or another of the traditional styles or genres.

The Dravidian languages are fourteen in number, and are spoken by more than seventy million people. Four groups (the four principal ones) have developed a literature: Tamil, Malayâlam, Kannari and Telugu.

Tamil

Tamil is spoken by some 20,000 people, in the south of India and along the east coast as far as Madras and beyond; it is also spoken in the northern part of Ceylon and in scattered settlements in East Asia and in Africa. Tamil literature is at once the richest and oldest in the Dravidian group; it goes back, very probably, to the first centuries of our era, although no datable literary text is earlier than the seventh. The inscriptions recently discovered in the region of Pondicherry (the site of Vìrapatnam) are from the first century. One must dismiss the fantastic datings indulged in by some Indian enthusiasts for Tamil, who are anxious to give their language a prestige, if they can, even greater than that of Sanskrit.

Tradition attributes the creation of Tamil literature to the sage Agastya, who is mentioned very early, namely in the *Rig-Veda*. He is supposed to have been the author of the first grammar. "Old Tamil," which has its origins in the seventh century, consists essentially of the cycle created by the *Sangam*, a sort of academy whose seat was at Madura, and that claimed the privilege of subjecting poetic output to a stringent control. As a matter of fact, the very existence of the *Sangam* is contested. (This is all the more so in the case of two earlier *Sangams* or *Sangam* periods, for it would mean making the origins fabulously ancient.) But the fact remains that we possess a considerable body of separate strophes in Old Tamil—said to number thirty thousand—of the panegyric genus, composed by bards in honor of the rulers they served. These strophes are grouped in eight anthologies, the *Eduttogais,* for the authorship of which a large number of names is put forward. In addition to these anthologies there are ten fairly long poems (or ten "idylls"), the shortest of which has 782 lines; they have a single title, *Pattupâddu,* and each is a kind of sung romance. There are also independent poems. Finally, the "minor" texts of the *Sangam* (called "minor" because the stanzas are very short) are a group of eighteen works, among which is the celebrated *Kural.*

This latter group as a whole is characterized first and foremost by the predominance of secular themes. Religion comes in only occasionally, as part of the setting; aspects of early Hinduism, possibly proto-Hinduism, crop up; so does the belief in the ancient Dravidian god of war, Muragan, and the terrifying goddess Korravai. A warlike Kâlî (no doubt the equivalent of Korravai) is described in the war poem *(parani)* entitled *Kalingattupparani,* in thirteen cantos, attributed to Jayangondâr, a poem celebrating the Cola invasion of Kulottunga I and therefore dated about 1100. But on the whole it is the romantic element that predominates: the expression of courtly and chivalrous sentiments, sometimes with a tinge of marked eroticism; social descriptions and accounts of festivals play some part, too. Another important aspect is the gnomic attitude: there are many stanzas conveying some precept of practical wisdom or worldly virtue, or containing the substance of some fable or other, or some more or less pointed instruction on the conduct of life. The artistic success of some of these short pieces is highly praised, particularly those that constitute the *Nâladi* and were arranged by Padumanâr: four hundred quatrains on the "three aims of life," apparently archaic in style and faintly tinged with Jainism. But by general agreement the first place of all goes to the *Kural,* the *"Holy Kural,"* as it is called (the word means "short piece"), by Tiruvalluvar. This is so perfectly

written as to be one of the great works of Indian antiquity, a
"fifth Veda," as the Tamils say. Its date is not easy to fix; some
put it about 500; tradition puts it at the end of the *Sangam* period, but such an affirmation hardly amounts to much. The
Kural is a collection of one thousand three hundred stanzas on
virtue, material prosperity and love, written in the form of
epigrams that are irreproachably pertinent and concise. The
nature of the material is human and universal; specifically or
exclusively Indian material hardly enters in. There are other
poems presented in the same fashion, written in a highly elabo-
rated style, which in point of artifice yield nothing to the Sanskrit *kâvya*.

Another significant body of work, though less homoge-
neous, and also less archaic, is the group of what we may call
"epic romances." These, unlike the foregoing works, which are
more or less indifferent where religion is concerned, display precise doctrinal preoccupations. There are two sets of these epic
poems; the more important, that of the long major poems, is
represented by five works, of which only three have come down
to us. The first of these is the *Silappadikâram*, by an unknown
author (apparently a Jain) disguised under a pseudonym. The
story is conventional enough: the passion of the head of a noble
family, Kovalan, for a courtesan, Mâdhavi, who causes him to
leave his faithful wife; various vicissitudes follow. The narrative is little more than a pretext for digressions on matters of
doctrine, and descriptions of all the Tamil kingdoms in turn.
The work is regarded as a masterpiece of elegant, harmonious
style. The second epic romance is still more important where
history and doctrine are concerned, though certainly of less
literary value. The author is Sâttanar of Madura; the title, *Mani-
mêkalai*, is the name of the daughter born of the illicit union
described in the preceding romance. The aim of the work is
edification; it follows the adventures of the girl, who, after
Kovalan's death, had been taken off to a Buddhist cloister by

her mother. The poem is in fact didactic, and Hindu attitudes are judged and condemned in the name of Buddhism. Finally, there is the *Jîvakachintâmani* (or, more briefly, *Chintâmani*), a poem in three thousand lines divided into thirteen cantos, written by a Jain ascetic called Tiruttutakkadêvar. This, a more recent work than the others (attempts have been made to prove that it is of the eleventh century), tells the story of a kind of Don Juan, a King of Jîvaka whose adventures always end in a happy marriage (whence the subtitle sometimes given to the *Chintâmani*, "The Book of Marriages"). The poem's charming episodes and graceful style insure it a high place in ancient literature.

To end our account of the ancient period, mention must be made of a versified Tamil grammar written at the height of the era, the *Tolkâppiyam;* the author, Tolkâppiyâr, is traditionally supposed to have been a pupil of Agastya. His treatise is of great value, giving elements of poetics and other learned matters as well as a grammatical account of the language. For practical purposes the *Tolkâppiyam* was replaced in the twelfth century (under Kolttunga III) by the *Nannûl*, a grammar by Pavanandi (a Jain), which is still regarded as authoritative.

Middle Tamil, which is already to be found in some of the works just described, begins in the seventh century and is remarkable for the predominance of religious subjects. It is considered to have reached its peak in the thirteenth and fourteenth centuries, a period regarded in southern India generally as having seen the "Shaiva awakening," although the origins of this awakening lie rather further back. Buddhism and Jainism found their progress checked more and more; subsequently Buddhism was pushed out of the subcontinent (maintaining its hold only in Ceylon), and Jainism was reduced to a few isolated groups that have subsisted until the present day. This was the result of the emergence of a succession of Shaiva and Vaishnaiva personalities who influenced the population by their preaching in verse. The pioneers were perhaps the "Holy Shaivaites," those known as the Nâyanârs, sixty-three in number. They are revered in all the temples of Shiva in Tamil territory, which still resound to their songs. On the literary plane, however, only three left definite traces. Appar (seventh century), his contemporary Sambandar and Sundarar or Sundaramûrti (at a slightly later period, under the Pallava king Dantivarman).

The first of these writers left poems that breathe an ardent, fanatical devotion; the second was an even more fanatical Brâhman (he is reputed to have approved the slaughter of eight thousand Jains who refused to be converted) but is less violent in his writings. The eight hundred hymns attributed to them were brought together to form the *Têvâram*, or "Divine Necklace," which was compiled in the tenth or eleventh century by Nambi Ândâr Nambi; this constitutes the first seven books of the "Tamil Veda," the *Tirumarai*. The four remaining books are the work of seven hundred and seventy "holy men" (not included in the ranks of the *Nâyanârs*). One of them, whose writings deserve a special place of honor, was Mânikkavâsagar (date uncertain; some people say he is earlier than Appâr, but that is unlikely). His *Tiruvâsagam*, the "Holy Word," is one of the gems of Tamil hymnology—exuberant, passionate poetry with a rich doctrinal background. To the same writer, who was the minister of one of the Pândya kings, we owe the *Tirukkôvai*, a poem with a double meaning, at once erotic and mystical, in four hundred stanzas.

The "Vaishnava Veda," also known simply as "the composition" (Skr. *prabandha*), in the highest sense of the word forms a counterpart to the Shaiva Veda. It is made up of the "four thousand hymns" *(Nâlâyiram)* that were collected in the eleventh century by Nâthamuni and were written by twelve holy people (one of them a woman): the Alvârs, whose period of activity extends from the seventh to the ninth century. They are regarded as *avatârs*, and a cult is devoted to them. The most famous of them is Nammâlvâr, to whom are attributed not only a considerable portion of the "Veda" (the third thousand, or *Tiruvâymoli*) but also a multitude of stanzas that attest a simple religious emotion devoid of polemical spirit, and therefore making a sharp contrast with the violence of Shaiva religious passions. Some readers place Nammâlvâr on a level with the greatest mystics of all ages. Whether one agrees or not, there is another Alvâr who must be placed almost as high as he: Tirumangai, who was contemporary with King Pallavamalla (eighth century); he was a master of controversy and apologetics. The legend of Krishna is represented by the *Tirumoli* of Periyâlvâr.

Although the worship of Vishnu was at least as important as that of Shiva, in Tamil-speaking territory, the Vishnuites used Sanskrit for theology and philosophy (this is the movement promulgating "qualified non-dualism," beginning with Nâthamuni and Yâmunachâryâ); the Vaishnava sect has nothing in Tamil to compare with what is found on the Shaiva side—the massive body of writings known as the *Shaivasiddhânta*. The oldest treatise in it is the short *Sivajñânabodam*, by Meykandâr (or Meykandadeva) a pious Vellâla of the beginning of the thirteenth century, whose work is the initial impulse from which there grows a vast religious literature, subdivided into schools. Among the works of Meykandâr's pupils, mention must be made of the authoritative versified form (the *Sivajnânasittiyâr*), by Arunandi, of the master's treatise; and various manuals and a collection of legends (the *Koyipurânam*), by Umâpati (early fourteenth century), who wrote in Sanskrit as well as Tamil. On a more popular level there is the activity of the Sittârs (=Siddha), or "doctors," whose hymns, written from the thirteenth century on and perhaps earlier, were collected into a *Shivavâkya*.

An impulse from a different direction, closer to Sanskrit models both in its subject matter and in its stylistic aspirations, gave birth to epic and Purânic poems: versions of the *Mahâ-*

Bhârata (three of which are known, the first of them dating perhaps from as early as the eighth century); versions of the *Râmâyana*, of which the most famous is that by Kamban, written
about 1180 (during the reign of Kulottunga III). In this, which
is known either as the *Kamba Râmâyana* (after the author's
name) or as the *Râmâvatâram*, Kamban uses an elegant and artificial style with which to give a free imitation of Vâlmîki's poem,
which he swells out to forty-eight thousand lines (the last part
was finished at a later period). There are also versions of the
Bhâgavata and other *Purânas*. But the "Purânic" genre also
engenders independent compositions known as the *Sthalap-
purânas*, whose materials are supplied by places of pilgrimage
and by local legends, and whose religious doctrine is infused
with *bhakti* and *tântrism*. A poem of a somewhat isolated type
is the very popular *Periyapurânam* of Sekkilâr (about 1100, in
the reign of Kulottunga I), an enormous versified biography of
the sixty-three Nâyanârs (notably the "three great ones") that
at the same time glorifies the Cola princes and their devotion to
Shiva. This work, which may perhaps owe something to the
epic biographies of the Jains, was regarded as an appendix to
the *Tirumurai*. There is also an abridged version in prose.

The modern period in Tamil begins in the sixteenth century, after a period of suspended animation. Religious works,
both Shivaite and Vishnuite, flourished. There are even works of
Christian propaganda written in Tamil, starting with the Jesuit
priest Joseph Beschi (d. 1747), who earned himself a place
equal to that of the Tamil classic authors. His *Life of St. Joseph*
in three thousand six hundred and fifteen stanzas, which appeared in 1724 under the title *Têmbâvani*, was freely influenced
by the ancient *Chintâmani* and the Tamil *Purânas*.

But the most interesting works, naturally enough, are the
secular ones. Prose, which had been comparatively neglected in
ancient times, now comes into the foreground. Contact with
traditional themes is maintained for a long time, it is true, at

least as regards the actual events of the narratives borrowed; such is the case in drama, for instance, of whose entry into Tamil literature we have no example earlier than the eighteenth century. In this field the modern tendency is connected with the name of Sambanda Mudaliar; and in other fields, with that of Subramania Bharathi, poet, storyteller and translator of the *Bhagavad-Gîtâ*. A fluent, readable prose, relieved of the burden of ancient rhetorical ornamentation, is that of Ârumuga Navalar, who was active both as an educator and as a propagator of the language. Ramalingam of Nammakâl, born in 1888, was a zealous apostle of Gandhi and expressed his zeal in his poetry. Among lyric poets of a later generation, names to be remembered are those of Desika Vinayagam Pillai and Bharati Dasan. Many translations into Tamil have been made, of both Indian and non-Indian works.

Finally, at all periods of their literary history the Tamils have made important contributions in the various technical disciplines, notably music, medicine, poetics, prosody and lexicography; we have already mentioned their work in grammar. Naturally, they show a varying degree of dependence on the Sanskrit works in the same fields, but there is no lack of works whose Sanskrit originals, if they had any, have disappeared.

Malayâlam

Malayâlam, which is spoken in Kerala, that is to say in the extreme south and southwest of India, is closely related to Tamil, and indeed is commonly considered to be only a Tamil dialect. Its literary relationship to Tamil is especially close. Its vocabulary is in some ways the more conservative of the two.

Its epigraphy begins in the tenth century; its literature, properly so called, in the thirteenth. The literature is extensive and is for the most part traditional and religious. Much of it is an imitation of Sanskrit style; the name for a mixed composition, partly in Sanskrit and partly in Malayâlam, is *manipravâla.* Thus there are several *Râmâyanas,* mostly of uncertain date, the oldest (a *Râmacharitra* by a poet named Mahârâja) having apparently been written in the thirteenth century; and a "Song of Krishna," by Cherusseri Nambûri, is thought to be of the sixteenth. There is a chronicle of Kerala that may have been written as early as the seventeenth century, containing folklore themes and, especially, dances or rather songs for dancing to; these, in common with the universal Indian tendency, frequently combine the sensual note with the mystical.

An original invention of the Malâyalams was *Kathâkali.* This is the name for a dramatic story told in an alternation of recitatives and lyrical dialogues, its subject taken from the old legends. The performance is held in the temple precincts during the numerous festivals of the Hindu calendar. The actors, who are professional rhapsodists, wear a highly developed makeup amounting in effect to a mask; expressiveness depends on the play of fingers and hands, on what are called the *mudrâs,* or "seals"; the use of certain key positions, varied with the help of several hundred complementary figurations, enables the actor to render not only emotions but also objects and even abstract ideas. The *mudrâs* of *kathâkali* are related to others that can be found in Southeast Asia, as far away as Java and Bali, and which probably came originally from India. The *kathâkali* style itself has taken root and flourished in various Indian provinces more or less distant from Malabar. Its origins may be ancient.

In modern times Malayâlam has been the medium of numerous novels and stories, and also of prose plays of which the subjects are usually social. In poetry there is a great name to be mentioned: that of Vallathol, who has successfully allowed popular feeling to infuse his verse; he is regarded as having initiated a new poetic form, whose further development cannot as yet be foreseen.

Kannari

Kannari is spoken over a considerable area in the south (the region of Mysore and that of southern Hyderabad) and the southwest. It has an abundant literature, beginning in the ninth century with an *Art of Poetry* in which earlier writers are mentioned. As usual, the inscriptions take us back rather further; the earliest dated one is from A.D. 450.

The Old Kannari period is dominated by Jain works and especially by the Sanskrit Great Epic, rehandled in Kannari versions with an edifying purpose in mind. Pampa, for example (tenth century)—later referred to as the "original Pampa," to distinguish him from a twelfth-century Pampa *"redivivus"*—produced a very free abridgement of a section of the *Mahâ-Bhârata,* the *Vikramârjuna-Vijaya* or *Pampa-Bhârata,* and also an *Adi-Purâna,* whose subject is the first of the "prophets" *(tîrthankara)* of Jainism. He is reputedly the greatest poet to have written in Kannari. Another important name is his slightly younger contemporary Ponna, who wrote about the sixteenth Tîrthankara. The last of the "Three Jewels" is Ranna, who lived in the time of Taila II; he adapted epic scenes and wrote *campus.* Pampa *redivivus* was the author of a *campû* in sixteen cantos that gives the Jain version of the legend of Râma, the *Râmachandra-Charitra-Purâna.* Various scientific works, grammars and lexicons were compiled in the same period.

Hindu inspiration established itself toward the end of the twelfth century, that is to say, at the beginning of the Middle Kannari period. This change was brought about by the zealous and indeed somewhat fanatical activity of a Shaiva sect, the Virashaivas, or, as they are still called, Lingâyats (who were active in Tamil territory, too)[1] Their founder, or rather re-

---

[1] Louis Renou, *The Nature of Hinduism* (New York: Walker and Company, 1962), chap. vi.

former, Basava, lived in the twelfth century and was the minister of King Kalachuri Bijjala (of Kalyânî). The sect honors the Nâyanârs and other Tamil holy men. The works attributed to Basava are written in simple prose, suitable for reading by the common people; they are *vachanas*, "sayings," short epigrams inculcating the need for belief in Shiva. Basava's adepts and successors, over two hundred in number, continued the writing of *vachanas* and signed them with their own "seals" *(mûdras)*. A parallel development is that of *vîrashaiva* lyricism, whose linguistic fulcrum (so to speak) is deliberately chosen from a more archaic stage of the language. Besides various works of propaganda—catechisms, versions of religious legends—there are lives of the sixty-three Nâyanârs, and an incredibly large quantity of *Purânas* and similar compilations (some of them in *campû* form) written to extol Basava and his miracles; one example is the *Basava-Purâna,* by Bhîmakavi (fourteenth century), which is thought to be the earliest of these works and which has a sequel in the *Cannabasava-Purâna,* by Virûpâksha Pandita (sixteenth century), idealizing the Master's nephew and collaborator, Cannabasava, in the same style.

There are also works of controversy, which are more technical in nature and which become more numerous in later periods, under the pressure of Vaishnava competition. The literary history of the Vaishnavas begins in the eleventh century, but at first, following Râmânuja, they wrote exclusively in Sanskrit. Vaishnava works in Kannari are rare until the sixteenth century, at which period an abundance of translations and new works sprang up; the Vijayanagar rulers fostered the movement, especially Chikkadeva Râya (1672-1704), who also patronized the writing both of a history of his realm and of a free version of *Ratnâvalî.* Whereas other Dravidian literatures begin declining in the seventeenth century, Kannari enters on a new upsurge of development in Mysore. This period is usually held (though without any great certainty to have seen the birth of a vast poem in praise of Krishna, the *Jaimini-Bhârata* of Lakshmîsha, which is vaguely related to a Sanskrit work of the same title; and there are also lyrics and various traditional forms of composition, some of them showing Jain influence.

The modern period has been equally active, and every kind of writing abounds. Prominent among the poets are K. V. Puttappa (praised for his limpid style), V. Sitamariah, Madhura Chenna ("the Kannari Blake") and Gokak; there are many more. There are also many novelists and short-story writers; and among the leading dramatists are T. P. Kailasam, who has been compared to Ibsen, and R. V. Jagirdar, whose specialty is social satire. Translations, technical works and written records of folklore have been appearing ever since ancient times.

Telugu

Telugu, which extends northward from Madras to the frontiers of Orissâ, is the language of 26 million people and is thus more widely spoken than any other Dravidian idiom; it is also the closest to Indo-Aryan, at least in vocabulary, and the furthest from Tamil. The first dated inscription is from 633.

The literature of Telugu (also known as Ândhra, from the name of the former kingdoms of the territory) makes its appearance in the eleventh century. It is associated with a recrudescence of Hinduism (in a Shaiva form) whose effect was to eliminate the influence of the Jains. The first major work is an abridgement of the *Mahâ-Bhârata*, by Nannayya Bhatta (eleventh century), who is also credited with the first Telugu grammar, the *Ândhrashabda-Chintâmani*. But Nannayya only got as far as translating the first two cantos and part of the third. It was Tîkkana (thirteenth century), the most gifted of all the poets in the Old Telugu period (he earned the epithet of "poet-Brahman"), who completed the version from cantos 4 to 18, while Yerrâpragada (fourteenth century), the last of the "big three," finished off the third canto and also adapted other works of the same kind. These three were the founders of the Telugu poetic tradition and initiated a broad literary development, which was at first *vîrashaiva* in tendency for the most part and then, from the thirteenth century on, became Vaishnava or simply secular. It included romances, and works on grammar, rhetoric, mathematics and so on. A large number of adaptations was made from the great Sanskrit texts; some of them depart very widely from the originals. One at least of the many adaptations from the *Purânas* is worth mentioning, that by Pôtana (fifteenth century), who wrote a popular, less concentrated version of the *Bhâgavata;* his powerful religious impulse and his impressive style has earned him a place as one of the best-loved authors in the language.

But the greatest name in this development is incontrovertibly that of Vêmana (second half of the fifteenth century?), a man of low birth, whose rough, simple poetry sounds a new note. He attacks Brâhmanic ritual and champions a worship free of idols and formal practices. He makes liberal use of social satire in his inspired, raggedly written poems, which at times display an outspoken realism. Vêmana's diction is natural and much freer from Sanskrit imitation than is that of his forerunners; but the scholarly tradition, as is shown by Telugu literature from the sixteenth to the eighteenth century inclusively, quickly regains command; there is a recrudescence of the *prabhanda* ("composition") style, which is equivalent to the Sanskrit *mahâkâvya* and to *mahâkâvya*'s worst excesses of linguistic preciosity; this period has been called "the age of despair." The Vijayanagar rulers take part in the movement, as patrons of poets and, in some cases, as poets themselves (e.g. Krishna Râya in the early sixteenth century); some of these rulers were scholars or instigated scholarly studies. Attention may be drawn, because of his exceptional adroitness, to Pingali Sûrana, who wrote among other things the *Kalâpûrnodaya,* a fairy-tale romance that is a distant imitation of the *Kâdambari.*

Telugu literary output in recent times has been considerable. The figure regarded as having initiated modern tendencies is Vîresalingam, a kind of social missionary who performed his task mainly by writing a multitude of propagandistic tracts, but who also set an example for artistic renewal with his poems, plays, novels, and translations from Sanskrit and English. His disciple Chilakamarti Lakshminarasimham, "the blind poet of the Ândhra country," specialized in plays and novels. Chronologically closer to us are the Kavulu brothers, known as the Heavenly Twins of Telugu literature, who, leading the life of wandering poets, have revived the folk tradition in poetry and give poetic improvizations. Gidugu Ramamurti Pantulu, a scholar rather than a writer, waged a successful struggle to insure that the form of Telugu used in education should be one close to the spoken language.

Telugu theatre has remained close to the soil. One of its permanent features is a sung recitation *(burrakathâ)* by three characters, one of whom has charge of the story while the two others make up the chorus, accompanying themselves on the Ândhra country's characteristic oblong drum. In the towns there is "street theatre," which is devoted mainly to the drama of maners; there is also a kind of puppet theatre in which leather dolls are used.

Part Four / The Modern Indo-Aryan Literatures

7 / THE MODERN INDO-ARYAN LITERATURES

General

The Modern Indo-Aryan languages, twenty-seven in number, are spoken by about 270 million people in India and Pakistan; some of these languages have spread beyond the subcontinent, being spoken in the Indian settlements scattered in East Asia and in South and East Africa. They are descended from Sanskrit, and their grammar is the result of a natural evolution from Sanskrit grammar in the direction of simplification and analysis (use of a periphrastic conjugation, creation of prepositions, and, more especially, of postpositions, and so on). The vocabulary is also of Sanskrit origin, though there is an influx of foreign elements, which varies in amount from language to language, the most notable of such contributions being the influx of Persian and Arabic elements caused by the Turko-Moslem invasions. On the other hand, there are few precise connections between any given Prâkrit that tradition assigns to a region of India, and the modern language spoken in that region. The change has taken place as if by a gradual transition from an almost undifferentiated *koinë* to the full development of the languages now existing, just like the transition from Vulgar Latin to the Romance languages.

The emergence of the modern languages dates from about the year 1000, with a difference of from one to three centuries in different instances. The process must have been aided (as must also the birth of the respective literatures) by the Moslem invasions; these caused a territorial fragmentation and, by a kind of self-protective mechanism, the establishment of new linguistic communities in accordance with new needs.

Few major literatures resulted. Three large groups must be seen as occupying the foreground: Hindi, Bengâlî and Marâthî, and five in a secondary position: Oriyâ, Panjabî, Gujratî and Assamese, while Urdû, which is only a variant of Hindi, stands in a place apart.

On the whole, the Sanskrit tradition exercised at least as great an influence as it did on the Dravidian group: it imposed traditional subjects, scholarly composition and a more or less artificial vocabulary; poetry predominated everywhere over prose. The situation changed, sometimes abruptly, when contact with English began at the start of the nineteenth century. Without abandoning their former approach to composition, the literatures started to become modern, and their respective languages moved away from ornateness toward simplicity; thought in general took a new turn. As a well-known Bengâlî writer has said, "With English, prose entered India and rhyme gave way to reason."

The Himalayan Languages

We can pass rapidly over the small groups of Himalayan languages. Kâshmîrî enters literature with the poetess and ascetic Lallâ (Lâl Ded) (sixteenth century), whose *Lallâvâkyanî* gives a living, sensitive rendering of Shaiva aspirations and

Kashmiri doctrines. After this comes the usual assortment of works drawing on the great mythological stories; there are, for example, an elegant adaptation of the Râmâyana (with some new episodes), and a *Marriage of Shiva,* in lofty style, both by the nineteenth-century poet Râzdân (Krishna Râjânaka). More important are the folk tales recited by professional storytellers, such as those made up by Hâtim; the improvised plays, many of them humorous; and the adroit rewriting of Persian poems on the part of the Moslem Mahmûd Gâmî (d. 1855).

The literature that the Gurkhas have created in Nepâlî (the language is also known as Parbatiyâ or Eastern Pahâri) is hardly known except for what was written in the nineteenth century; imitations of the great works of the past, and also a few original works, such as those credited to Bhânu Bhakta (b. 1812). Historical chronicles are reported to have been written before that time. In Nevârî (a dialect of Pahâri, impregnated with Tibetan and Burmese vocabulary) there are Buddhist translations, a version of the *Tales of the Throne,* and finally inscriptions, of which the earliest may date from the fourteenth century.

Hindi

With its dialectal variants, Hindî forms an impressive group that is spoken in northern India and extends from the Himâlayas southeast to beyond the river Taptî, as far as the eastern marches of the Deccan. Westward, it extends into a wide area of the middle Indus Basin; and eastward, beyond Benares.

It is the day-to-day idiom of about 125 million people, but the dialects it includes represent a considerable diversity of levels in linguistic development; such are Râjasthânî to the west (Râjputânâ), Avadhî to the east (region of Allahâbâd/Benares), Chattîsgarhî to the southeast, and finally, "Western" Hindî or Hindî proper, whose principal dialect is Braj, spoken at Âgrâ,

Delhî and Mathurâ. However, it is not Western Hindî or Braj that has served as the common language but a rather obscure dialect from the foothills of the Himalâyas, known in Europe from the eighteenth century on as "Hindustani." This dialect exists in two varieties One of them is Islamicized: while the grammar has remained Indian in character, the vocabulary, particularly as regards nouns, is very largely Arabic and Persian (the script is Persian, too). This variety is called Urdû, the "(language of) the Horde (the people of the military camp and the bazaar)." It is spoken in some Hindu milieux, but in general it is the Moslems' language: not of all the Moslems in India, but of those in the Hindî zone and at Hyderâbâd. Another form of Hindustani is literary Hindî, which, having spread rapidly in northern India during the last fifty years or so, was promoted to the position of the pan-Indian national language shortly after independence (1949). Its vocabulary, unlike that of Urdû, is mainly Sanskrit, and in some circles there is even an urge for its total reconversion to Sanskrit. The term "Hindustani" is tending to fall into disuse. As for Urdû, its future in India appears to be threatened; it will doubtless survive for some time, but be spoken only by Moslems living inside the Indian Union.

The origins of Hindî literature are said to lie in the eighth century. But the first text of any importance that has been preserved is the epic (in sixty-nine cantos and one hundred thousand lines) of Chand Bardâî of Lahore (twelfth century), which is written in Western Hindî and relates the exploits of the last Hindu king of Delhî, Prithirâj; its title is *Prithirâj Râsau*. But we know this work only through a later version, of which the nucleus, at most, is ancient; moreover the language is obscure and the historical accuracy of the narrative doubtful The poem seems to have been the culmination of a whole body of work whose purpose was to glorify the Râjputs and their endless struggles against the Moslems; the authors were the companies of bards (*cêrans* or *bhats*) who were maintained at the ruler's courts. There is a short Râjput correspondence that can be accepted as authentic; it dates from the twelfth century. Later, in the field of the lyric, attention must be drawn to the poems of a fourteenth-century Persian, Amîr Khusro, written in pure Avadhî.

Passing to the religious field, nothing certain, either as to authenticity or as to date, can be found among the works in prose and verse attributed to Gorakhnâth (Gorakshanâtha, eleventh century; Eastern Bengal?), who founded or reformed a Shaiva sect (the Kânphatayogîs) but whose very existence cannot be established definitely. In any case, what we possess of his in Hindî is of no great importance. Vishnuism, on the other hand, left a much deeper impression, through the sermons of Râmânanda and everything that followed from them. A Brâhman from Allahâbâd, Râmânanda formed a sect of Râma-worshipers in the fifteenth century; he left no writings of his own (except one hymn, the only composition to have been preserved under his name), but his disciples and others influenced by him initiated an enormous devotional literary movement. Tradition has it that one of his twelve disciples was Kabîr, who perhaps owes even more to Gorakhnâth. The adopted son of a Moslem weaver in Benares, Kabîr (1440-1518) aspired to see Hinduism and Islam amalgamated into a single monotheistic faith, without images or formal practices; he called himself "the son of Allah and Râma." His life is legendary, and a death surrounded by miraculous circumstances was attributed to him. It is probable that he did not become an ascetic but remained an artisan and founded a family. The authentic collection of his utterances, which he dictated to his pupil Bhagojî, is the *Bîjak*, the "Account," written in an archaic, rather abstruse Hindî. He is not a graceful writer, but his maxims are often striking. The faith they teach is simple: God is for everyone, everyone can reach salvation through faith and direct union with the divine. Some of his verses made their way into the *Granth* (see below), and his collection was partly translated into English by Tagore, from a Bengâlî version.

Kabîr was freely imitated by Nânak (1469-1538), who founded the Sikh sect.[1] His hymns and those of his nine successors (who, with him, are the ten "masters" of the Sikh church) were collected later; at first by the fifth *guru*, Arjun, who in 1604 made the *Granth*, the "Book," out of them, adding poems from other sources and dividing the whole according to the thirty-one musical tones, on the model of the arrangement of the *Rig-Veda*. The work was subsequently completed by the tenth *guru*, Govind. It contains altogether fifteen thousand stanzas, mostly in Hindî: liturgical pieces, hymns, panegyrics and isolated verses, with a supplement called the *Dasham Granth*, "Book of the tenth *(guru)*," in consequence of which the old *Granth* became known as the "Original *Granth*." Nânak and his imitators helped themselves freely from the mass of earlier mystical poetry, the Bhagats and the Sûfîs; their religion, like Kabîr's, is a simple monotheism that lays stress on ethical values and has nothing to do with the militant, authoritarian doctrine of the Sikhs in later times.

There were many other examples of "sectarian" development in the Hindî zone between the sixteenth and eighteenth centuries, and, correspondingly, many other doctrinal expositions and mystical compositions. But one man's work towers over the rest, and indeed dominates the whole of the religious literature of modern India: that of Tulsîdâs. Tulsîdâs, a Brâhman of Râjpur (1532-1623) who became an ascetic at an early age, lived and died at Benares; he spent his days preaching and singing, teaching the Vaishnava faith and urging tolerance and unity. His aim seems to have been to group the vital forces in Hinduism about the theme of Râma and to draw from them the ingredients of a living faith; one that would safeguard tradi-

[1] Louis Renou, *The Nature of Hinduism* (New York: Walker and Company, 1962), chap. vi.

tion and maintain its own identity against the threat of external forces. To this end he had no hesitation in making use of the rival doctrines of Krishnaism and Shivaism; his role was that of a unifier and in no way that of a doctrinaire. The works attributed to him are numerous, most of them in Avadhî, a few in Braj or even Sanskrit; they comprise lyrical poems, whose technique is learned in some cases and popular in others; there is, for example, the *Gîtâvalî,* a series of stanzas for singing, on the life af Râma. But there is one outstanding poem, the *Râmcharitmânas,* or "Mountain Lake (which means in effect the quintessence) of the life of Râma"; it is a free adaptation of the *Râmâyana,* and is usually known as the *Râmâyana* of Tulsî. The writer has drawn on other Sanskrit sources besides Vâlmîki; he has retained the essential features of the legend, but the purpose he pursues is very different from that of Vâlmîki. For Tulsîdâs, Râma is the supreme god, and salvation comes only through absolute faith in Râma; Bharata, Râma's brother, is the model of the devout man, a new type of man created by *bhakti;* the effects of *bhakti* are illustrated by events, and all other events are illusory, the products of *mâyâ.* The legendary narrative is exploited with unequal success; everything in the poem has an edifying purpose. But from time to time the poet has described something just for the pleasure of doing so, and this makes some parts of his work, notably the second canto (*Ayodhyakanda),* wonderfully beautiful. The attraction of his style is heightened by a subtle use of meters and rhymes and by his correct and vigorous language; these virtues have earned for Tulsîdâs his fame as the creator of modern Hindî. However, the work owes its success not so much to its literary merits as to the serene spirit and lofty religious feeling that emanate from it; though it is true at the same time that the hearer does not separate these aspects from the storyteller's art by which they are adorned, and which is so pleasing to the ear. Throughout northern India the *Râmcharitmânas* is still read and recited

daily, and has been for more than three centuries; it is, as someone has written, the Bible of more than a hundred million
people.

Krishnaism has no comparable work to show. Its theology,
in the work of Vallabha, who is important both as a founder
of the sect and as a learned teacher of *Vedânta,* keeps up the
use of Sanskrit, prompted perhaps in this by the example of the
Bhâgavata-Purâna. But Vallabha's direct disciples, among
whom is his son Bitthalnâth (who succeeded him as head of the
sect in 1530), used Hindî; they are called the "eight seals" because they are regarded as the masters of the Braj language.
The most highly reputed of them is Sûrdâs, who composed innumerable chants *(bhajans)* to Krishna and Radha; these were
collected under the title of *Sûrsâgar.* He lived from 1483 to 1563,
mainly at Agra; he was blind. Many regard him as the greatest
name in Hindî lyricism.

The Canon of the Sikhs was enriched by the incorporation
of the Hindî hymns of the poet Nâmdev, from Mahratta territory, and his compatriot Trilocan. Their hymns are less remarkable than those of the famous Mîrâbâî, Princess of Jodhpur (sixteenth century), who wrote sometimes in Hindî and sometimes
in Gujrâtî. She is said to have abandoned her kingdom for love
of Krishna, and to have died at the foot of the statue of the god
whose bride she considered herself to be. Her ardent, simple
poems are still very well known today—even among shepherds,
and dancing girls, and the holy men of the little country shrines.
But for literary merit they cannot compare with those of Sûrdâs.

To complete our survey of the religious field in Hindî, we
must mention *Padumâvatî,* a sort of mystical epic written in
Avadhî, *circa* 1540, by a Moslem of Oudh, Malik Muhammad
Jâyasî (of Jais): a work full of the feudal traditions and heroic
legends of Râjputânâ, which relates the adventures of Pad-
mâvatî (Padminî), the wife of a *râjâ* of Chîtôr. A curious feature
is that it is written according to the canons of Sanskrit rhetoric.

The most prominent seventeenth-century work is the *Bhakta-mâlâ* of Nabhâdâs, in Western Hindî: the history of the Vaishnava holy men, summed up in one hundred and eight stanzas whose style is so concentrated that they need a commentary to make them intelligible.

The sixteenth and seventeenth centuries are the Golden Age of Hindî; the literature of that period shows a profusion that has been compared with that of early Buddhism, and that has been called an "enchanted garden" because of its brilliant images and its beauties of style.

The secular literature (or relatively secular, as we ought rather to say) stands out less; but it was nonetheless actively cultivated. Panegyrics, chronicles and genealogies in verse or prose continue the traditions of bardic poetry until the end of the Mogul period. The lyric properly so called comes to birth later, under Akbar (1556-1605); this enlightened monarch made his court a center of poetry, as many of the sovereigns of antiquity had done. He instigated translations from Hindî into Persian and vice versa. Even Moslems (as, for example, the author of *Padumâvatî*) practice the subtleties of Sanskrit or Hindî composition. Even under Aurungzeb in the seventeenth century, when conditions were unfavorable to the Hindu tradition, some support for the poets was still forthcoming. The Brâhman Keshavdâs (1555-1617), under Akbar and his successor Jahângîr, produced poems containing the strictest rhetoric; he was also a remarkable exponent of poetics, in his *Rasikprayâ* and *Kavipriyâ*, both of which are decorated with a number of stanzas, religious (Krishnaite) and profane, composed by the author. A little later, Bihârîlâl, with his "Seven Hundred Stanzas" (1662), rivaled the devices of Sanskrit *kâvya;* his collection is regarded as a masterpiece of its kind; and its content (which, it is true, is no more than a pretext for composition) is quite clearly taken from the worship of Krishna.

The modern period in Hindî begins with the second half

of the eighteenth century. The established literary species, particularly in religious poetry, maintain their position, but both form and subject matter undergo a gradual renewal. The creator of modern "high Hindî" is considered to be Lallû Lâl (early nineteenth century), a Gujrâtî Brâhman who imitated various Sanskrit texts in his supple, adroit prose; his *Premsâgar* (1804-1810), imitated from the Tenth Book of the *Bhâgavata,* enjoyed immense popularity. Prose was also the chosen medium of Dayânand Sarasvatî (1824-83), who founded the Âryasamâj,[2] and of his inner circle of disciples; but his impetuous verbosity, embracing theological and social themes, is far from having any pretensions to literary quality. In more recent times the name of Premchand (d. 1933), who wrote in Urdû to begin with, stands unrivaled; a highly gifted writer of novels and stories dealing with popular and rural life, he enriched the written language with a plentiful fund of dialectal words. Mention must also be made of Harishchandra of Benares, "the Moon of India" (d. 1885), a critic and historian who is also esteemed for his love-poems, which are written in Braj.

As in most of the modern Indian languages, the drama as a literary form developed late; and, while subject to traditional influences, it has been more accessible on the whole to new ideas. Jayasankar Prasad (who is also known as a philosophical poet) devoted his energies to the historical play. In the contemporary period Prithvi Raj Kapur, a professional actor, has earned himself a large following: in his *Divar* ("The Wall") he dramatizes the conflict between Hindu and Moslem; in *Pathan,* he describes family hatreds corrupting the friendship between a Khan and a high-born Hindu.

Since the rise of linguistic nationalism, and especially since independence, Hindî has been rapidly enriching itself with all the manuals and technical books that will help it to fulfill its role as a great social and cultural language.

[2] Renou, *The Nature of Hinduism,* chap. viii.

Urdû

With the literature in Urdû (which, in connection with poetry, is also called *rêkhta)* we shall deal briefly. Although this literature came into being in India and is therefore part of the Indian heritage, it is nonetheless a foreign literature by virtue of its mode of expression, the subjects of which it treats, and the spirit in which it treats them. And its prosody is alien to the Indian mind.

Its origins do not take us back far. Ancient Urdû is almost exclusively poetic; and the first poet of any importance is Walî, who flourished at Aurangabad in the latter part of the seventeenth century; it was he who established Urdû at Delhi; it had hitherto been an obscure tongue, confined to the Deccan. The classical writers of Urdû are Sandâ (of Delhi) and Mîr Taqî, of Âgrâ (eighteenth century); vigorous temperaments both of them, who distinguished themselves in the lyric and, on occasion, in satire. The school of Âdil and Allâhî and Qutb-Shâhî attracted the court poets and developed an art of acute verbal dexterity; at the same time they taught the various kinds of subservience proper to a courtier's life. The last representative of this tradition who is of any value is Zafar (first half of the nineteenth century), whose delicate love poems form a contrast to the often scabrous note struck by his predecessors. "Zafar" is a pseudonym; the writer was none other than Bahadur II Shah, the last of the line of the monarchs of Delhi.

The school of Lucknow, founded after the downfall of the sultans of Delhi, is devoted, as was earlier poetry in Urdû, to the learned, artificial way of composition, but it does let natural emotion break through here and there. The poems of Ghâlib (d. 1869) are entirely in Persian. Amânat (d. 1858) is the author of a play *(Indarsabhâ)* after which a whole group of playwrights is named.

Literary circles and writers are scattered after the Mutiny

(1857); the most active center thenceforth is Hyderâbâd, with Hâli, a "national" poet who was a pupil of Ghâlib, Azad (a nature poet above all), and others, such as Sarur (a specialist in the portrayal of emotion). The most notable writer is Iqbâl of Sialkot (1876-1938), in whom the immemorial mystical tendency is combined with modern aspirations; he is regarded as the national poet, and a kind of spiritual father, of Pakistan. Sayyid Ahmad Khan has written commentaries on the Koran, social chronicles, and Moslem propaganda works. Among recent dramatic writers, mention should be made of Khvaja Ahmed Abbas, whose play *Zubeida* is the story of a girl who casts off the veil to join a team of rescue workers in an epidemic, of which she herself finally becomes a victim.

Western Indian Languages

We need say little here about Sindhî, which is spoken in the lower Indus Basin. A prominent part in its ancient literature is played by the popular ballads that, arising no one quite knows when, were revived at the beginning of the eighteenth century in the "Book of the Shah" by Sayyid Abd-ul-Latîf, an enormous collection divided into thirty-five "melodies" and showing strong Islamic influence. Contemporary writing in Sindhî is said to be both varied and extensive, but no one name stands out and no sketch can be given of it.

Panjâbî literature (upper Indus Basin) begins with the compilation of the *Granth,* which contains poems in Panjâbî; some of these are attributed to writers from other linguistic areas, such as Kabîr, Nâmdev and Nânak. This is the Golden Age of Panjâbî literature. The predominating tendencies at this time are, on the one hand, Sikh influence (which is still dominant today), and, on the other, Sûfic influence, which guides the Moslem writers. There are also ballad versions of folk legends, such as the tale of the girl Hîr and her lover Rânjhâ, and the various obstacles with which their love is faced.

The seventeenth century is marked by a decadence; the eighteenth, by a revival, under Ranjit Singh. At present the most widely read writer seems to be Bhai Vîr Singh, who is particularly praised for an allegorical poem, *Rânâ Sûrat Singh* (1905), in thirty-five cantos, which the Sikhs rank on a level with their Holy Scripture.

Oral songs, especially in the Multânî dialect, have been collected. Among them are some women's songs, at once realistic and very beautiful, which describe a kind of ritual of marriage.

Gujrâtî literature (Kâthiâwâr and the surrounding districts) is the most important literature in this group. The most remarkable works have long been those produced in the Jain community; these, indeed, are the most significant of the Jain's contributions to literature, not counting their work in Sanskrit. They include complete translations of the Jain Canon, commentaries and adaptations of many ancient texts, and a special genre: the *Râsâs*, little tales written with an edifying purpose, whose origins may go back to the fourteenth century. Such tales are still composed today.

In the religious field, another contribution is that of the Pârsî community, who follow the ancient Zoroastrian religion. Their achievements include a considerable number of translations from Mazdean works, and, in modern times, a whole independent literature; in the latter are a number of secular works, such as plays adapted from Shakespeare, and historical and social plays and novels.

On the Hindu side we see, in the fifteenth century, the hymns of Narsimha Mehtâ, to whom more than twenty-five thousand stanzas are attributed; in the sixteenth, the Gujrâtî poems of Mîrâbâî, who has been mentioned already. Literature regains its impetus in the second half of the seventeenth century with the poetry of the goldsmith Akhâ, whose adroitly written verses are as much at home when describing the doctrines of Shankaryan non-dualism as when scourging worldly society and its ways. Premânand (seventeenth-eighteenth centuries), a Brâhman of Baroda, handles the epic and Purânic legends over again in dramatic versions, and does it brilliantly; he also makes use of Gujrâtî themes. Later, Dayârâm (d. 1852), a Brâhman who was a devotee of Vallabha, revives the religious lyricism of the sect of Krishna in his ardent verse.

Contemporary literature of some significance has been written in most of the available genres. The foundation of "modern Gujrâtî" is attributed to Narmadâshankar (d. 1886) of Surat, a poet and historian (he wrote among other things a history of the world). The nationalistic tendency, which can be felt in nearly all the literature of the period, comes to fruition in the work of Dalpatrâm (d. 1896), who was the adapter of one of Aristophanes' comedies and the mainstay of a Gujrâtî literary society founded by a Scotsman, Forbes, in 1848. The first novel of any importance is *Karan Ghelo* (1868), by Nandshankar Tuljâshankar, which is about the last Hindu king of Gujrât; the best known is *Sarasvatîchandra,* by Govardhanrâm (d. 1907), a kind of epic of the modern world, whose reputation has spread far beyond the borders of Gujrât. A prose writer of renown, who has been equally prolific in several kinds of writing—history, essays and drama, not to mention his activities in politics and education—is K. M. Munchi, whose career began about 1911.

A talented dramatic author is C. C. Mehtâ; among his works are *Narmad,* a play about the life of the Gujrâtî poet of that name, and, in a very different field, *Ag-Gari,* which is about life and conditions among railway workers.

And, of course, we must not forget the written work of Gandhi (Mohandâs Karamchand Gândhî): his newspaper articles, his letters, his autobiography. All these, in a style stripped of artifice, did much for the diffusion of Gujrâtî at the same time as they contributed (in how large a degree most people know) to founding the destinies of modern India.

Marathi

Marâthî (Mahratta) is spoken in Mahârâshtra territory (Bombay and the region south of it, and north and northeast as far as the heart of Central India) by no less than twenty-two million people. The beginnings of the literature may take us back as far as the end of the twelfth century, when the didactic poems of Mukundarâja gave a popularized exposition of *Vedânta* themes. But this dating must be regarded with great caution. The first important writer is Jñâneshvar (also known as Jñândev or Jñânobâ), who was born near Punâ (Poona). His main work is a free commentary, in ten thousand stanzas, on the *Bhagavad-Gîtâ;* it was finished in 1290 and is called, after its author, the *Jñâneshvari.* He was the founder of literary Marâthî; the depth of his inspiration and the somewhat abrupt beauty of his language have earned him the title of "the Dante of Mahratta territory." We are also indebted to him for a collection of twenty-eight *Abhangs* (literally "not-broken")—that is to say, short hymns inspired by the *Bhâgavata.*

In the late thirteenth and early fourteenth centuries (if the traditional dating is accepted; but many scholars distrust it), the religious poet Nâmdev is of some importance; he wrote numerous *Abhangs,* of which several (in Hindî versions) found their way into the *Granth;* he sings the glories of Vithobâ or Vitthal, the Marâthî form of Vishnu. He is sometimes thought to have been influenced by Kabîr; and there is a tradition that he was a pupil of Jñâneshvar. Another name deserving mention is Eknâth, a Brâhman of Paithan who lived in the second half of the sixteenth century, wrote *Abhangs* and translated parts of the *Bhâgavata.* Like Mukundarâja and Jñâneshvar, he is a "non-dualist" whose writings reflect the tendencies of the Shankaryan school.

But the greatest Marâthî poet is undoubtedly Tukârâm

(1607-49) of Dehu, a *shûdra* of the grain merchants caste, who became a wandering ascetic and devoted his life to chanted preaching *(kîrtana)*. The thousands of *Abhangs* he left, or at least that are attributed to him, bear witness to a mystical feeling that puts him among the greatest; he represents the culmination of the *bhakti* influence in western India. His verse is simple and direct; people of every class and every kind of education can find food for thought in it without difficulty.

Religious writing subsequently diminishes. On the score of literary fecundity we must mention Shrîdhar (seventeenth-eighteenth centuries), a Brâhman of Pandharpur whose writings either glorify Tukârâm or else interminably rehandle the great Epic and the *Purânas*. Mahîpati (eighteenth century), an imitator of Tukârâm, also enjoys a reputation for his semi-fictitious lives of the Marâthî holy men. But the most highly esteemed writer in the eighteenth century was Moropant (Mayûra), a subtle, scholarly artist who enriched Marâthî poetry with refinements imitated from Sanskrit (he also wrote in Sanskrit himself); he is known particularly for the use he made of the endless stock of material provided by the legendary epic.

Marâthî historical writing is more remarkable than that of most other Indian provinces, owing to the extraordinary expansion of Mahratta territory brought about by the conquests of Shivâjî (1627-80). Shivâjî, moreover, tried to attract Tukârâm to his court; and a profound impression was made on him by another contemporary, Râmdâs, who had founded a sect and was the author of poems of a Vedantic stamp. Political effervescence brought to birth a large quantity of accounts in prose or verse: the *bakhars* (historical chronicles) and *povâdâs* (martial ballads). Erotic lyrics (the *lâvanîs)* also flourish in this period; so do gnomic poetry and imaginative storytelling.

In the contemporary period, in addition to nationalistic works such as those of the famous Tilak (who also figured as a scholar and wrote a modernistic commentary on the *Bhagavad-*

Gîtâ, the *Gîtâharasya*), there is an ample choice of novels, essays on various subjects, and poems. The theatre is largely dominated by historical subjects; authors and audiences take pride in recounting their people's glorious past. There are also plays on social subjects (for instance, those of H. N. Apte, who is also known as a novelist of talent); some of these (such as those of Ram Ganesh Gadkari, alias Govindagraj) are humorous. And the influence of Ibsen and Shaw has stimulated the writing of naturalistic plays (such as those of Varerkar).

Eastern Indian Languages

Oriyâ. Inscriptions attest the existence of Oriya (the language of Orissâ in southern Bengal, between the domains of Bengali and Telugu) from the thirteenth century on, but the literature goes back no further than the fifteenth century. There are folk songs, on the one hand; and on the other, the usual rehandlings of the Sanskrit Epic and the *Bhâgavata*. The dominant tendency is religious—connected with the worship of Krishna, to be precise. The center of devotion is the famous temple of Vishnu Jagannâtha (the "Juggernaut" of early European accounts) at Purî. It was in Orissâ that the great Bengali reformer Chaitanya obtained his most numerous following, and at Purî that he spent the greater part of his life. The influence of the Chaitanyan movement can be seen in the works of a group of poets who write in the tradition of the sect of Krishna, notably Dînakrishnadâsa (second half of the sixteenth century), whose *Rasakallola*, in thirty-four cantos, describes the life of the youthful Krishna among the milkmaids.

At the beginning of the eighteenth century a more modern trend manifests itself in the work of Upendrabhanja, who was *râjâ* of Gumsur. Although he continues in the religious vein of his predecessors, and devoutly describes the Purî temple ceremonies, he also introduces a secular element with his epic romances (*Chitralekhâ, Lâvanyavatî* and so on)—stories of love and gallantry, written in a sophisticated style well suited to accommodate the preciosities of Sanskrit. This type of poem was felicitously imitated more than once; an example is the love-romance *Premakalâ,* by Abhimanyu Sâmantasimhâra (d. 1806). His contemporary Brajanâtha Barajenâ, describes in his *Samarataranga* the victory of the *râjâ* of Dhenkanal over the Mahrattas.

In the present day, which is rich in talent, one of the best prose writers is reputedly Râdhânâth Rây, with his studies of nature and his descriptions of the life of princes, and (in *Durbar*) his satirical observation of manners and morals; while in his Mahâyâtra he has turned an epic theme (the death of the Pândavas) to curious account by using it as a vehicle of social polemic. Madhusûdan Rao, a writer of excellent stories, is also a mystical poet.

Popular poetry is represented by religious odes (*bhajana*) intended to be recited or sung to the accompaniment of tambourines and dancing (*kîrtana*); by prayers (*janana*); and by love songs (*sangîta*). And there are poems called *chautishâs* in which the stanzas begin respectively with the letters of the alphabet taken in order (Dînakrishnadâsa had established a precedent for this), to a possible total of thirty-four stanzas (*chautishâ* means "thirty-four").

Assamese. In Assam we find at first only an oral "literature"—ballads, and the folk songs of shepherds and mountain-dwellers—whose origins lie in some unidentifiable period of the past. Literature proper begins in the fifteenth century with Shankaradeb, a Vaishnava reformer who founds the sect of the Mahâpurushiyas; he is a disciple of Chaitanya. His compositions are poems for singing and dancing (*kîrtana*) to the glory of Krishna, and an adaptation of the *Bhâgavata.* Later names to be remembered are those of Mâdhava Deva and his contemporary

Râmasarasvati (Ananta Kandali); the second of these translated the Epic.

In more recent periods there are numerous adaptations of Sanskrit works, especially in the religious field and the medical. There are also historical annals, the *bâranjis.*

Modern tendencies begin manifesting themselves with the appearance of English romanticism, to whose influence Assamese writers have reacted in varying degrees. Named as one of the best writers of today is Lakshminâth Bez Baruah, who is regarded as the founder of the new school and has made his mark in several different genres. In his wake comes Chandrakumar Agarvalla, a romantic poet with a tendency toward mysticism. Another modern literary figure is Hemchandra Gosvami, a prose writer and a talented lyrical poet.

There are some fifty plays in Assamese whose subjects are taken from heroic legend; some of these plays are survivors from the ancient dramatic repertory.

Bengali

The oldest specimens of the Bengali language—which is spoken by an enormous population, 55 million—are the forty-seven mystical songs known as *Charyâpadas,* which were discovered in 1907; they are thought to have been composed in the tenth and eleventh centuries, and may be the earliest datable examples of literature in any Indo-Aryan language. They were translated into Tibetan in the thirteenth century. They are inspired by the Sahajiyâ school of esoteric Buddhism; the authors, twenty-two in number, are reckoned among the four hundred and twenty-four *siddhas* (holy men) of Nepalese and Tibetan tradition. The commentary is in Sanskrit.

Later comes the *Chûnya-Purâna* of Ramâî Pandita, a work the date of which is hard to determine and which belongs to the literature issuing from the cult of Dharma, a sort of compromise between Hinduism and Buddhism: a mass of poems, called *Dharmamangalas,* or "Glorifications of Dharma," were composed in honor of the god Dharma and of Lâu Sen (eleventh century), king of Maina, who assumed the task of propagating this curious religion. There are, finally, popular legends in plenty from the same period until the fifteenth century and perhaps later, that is to say, in what is known as "Middle Bengali": the stories of Chând the merchant and those of Kâlaketu the hunter, and the Buddhist narratives of King Gôpichandra and others, all bearing witness to the Bengalis' inexhaustible gift for storytelling. It must be added that the circumstances in which these texts have been preserved often leave much to be desired; the same is true of the early Bengali gnomic poetry, which consists of maxims illustrated by parables.

The opening of the classical period can be fixed at the beginning of the fifteenth century, with the emergence of a succession of authors of high importance. The first of them, if we can trust the tradition that places him at the end of the fourteenth century, is Chandîdâs, a Brahman who was initially of the *shâkta* persuasion, attached to the temple of Chandî (whence his name) at Nannûr. Some think he was an adept of the Sahajiyâ cult; whether this be so or not, he soon became a worshiper of Krishna and sang of the loves of Krishna and Radha in ardent poetry, insisting on the necessity of feelings purged of all common desire. His work, the manuscript of which was not discovered until 1961, is entitled *Shrîkrishnakîrtana* and was perhaps written about 1450. It must be distinguished from that of another Chandîdâs, "Chandîdâs the Poor," whose date is about 1600.[3]

A contemporary of Chandîdâs is Vidyâpati Thâkur of Bihâr. As well as writing works of some importance in Sanskrit he composed in Maithilî a long series of songs that caused him

[3] There is a study of this poet and mystic in A. K. Coomaraswamy, *The Dance of Shiva* (rev. ed.; New York: Farrar, Straus and Cudahy, 1957).

to be called "the new Jayadeva"; he celebrates the themes of the Krishna-worshipers, in the dual key of eroticism and mysticism that became traditional in such writing from the time of the *Gîtagovinda*. Maithilî as a language is independent from Bengali; it belongs to the Bihârî group; but it carries a strong infusion of Bengali words, and all Vidyâpati's links are with Bengal, where his works attained enormous widespread popularity; some eight hundred ballads under his name have been collected, most of them more elaborately written than are the poems of Chandîdâs.

Another Bihârî writer of some importance was Umâpati Dhara, who probably came from Tirhut; he, too, wrote poems in honor of Krishna; some of them are interpolated in a play in Sanskrit that he also wrote. His date is disputable, and his works were not published until comparatively recently.

As in many other linguistic domains, a large place in the picture must be reserved for translations or adaptations of the great texts of antiquity. Thus in the fourteenth century (though no doubt there were other works of the same kind before) we have Krittivâs Ojhâ's free rendering of the *Râmâyana*, simply but elegantly written; a very popular work which has caused its competitors to be forgotten. The *Mahâ-Bhârata* reappears in the version of Kâshîrâm Dâs (seventeenth century); the *Purânas* reappear, too (especially certain parts of them, such as the *Chandîmâhâtmya* and the Tenth Book of the *Bhâgavata*) in a host of translations or imitations; this has been called the "Purânic renaissance." Ancient trends are often enriched by the addition of Chaitanyist influence.

The name of Chaitanya[4] dominates all others in the sixteenth century. Krishna Chaitanya Deva (1485-1533), a Brahman from Nadiyâ, traveled through all Bengal and Orissâ, preaching faith in Krishna and founding a religion based on

[4] Renou, *The Nature of Hinduism*, chap. vi.

ecstatic love; his death was surrounded with mystery and he was immediately raised to the rank of a saint. Though his own written work is slender in quantity, the movement of collective devotion that he started blossomed, even during his lifetime, in a number of works in Sanskrit and Bengali. The latter include treatises on dogmatics and ritual (apparently regarded as subordinate to those in Sanskrit) but also, and much more prominently, Lives of Chaitanya in verse, for which there was an incredible demand. There are, for example, the *Chaitanya-Bhâgavata* of Vrindâvan Dâs, and the *Chaitanya-Charitâmrita* (1582) of Krishnadâs Kavirâj (b. at Jhâmâlpur), which became the authoritative work; many devotees know it by heart.

Lyrical poetry of the kind started by Chandidas and Vidyâpati was carried on for two or three centuries in Brajbulî, a more or less artificial dialect that is undoubtedly composed of Old Maithilî modified by an influx of Bengali. The usual theme is the legend of Krishna and Radha. There are some two hundred poets of this sort (including even Moslems), the most prominent names being those of Govinda Dâs and Jñâna Dâs. As a rule the poems were collected in anthologies.

The cult of *shakti*, long suppressed by this powerful upsurge of Krishnaism, regains the upper hand in the work of Mukundarâm Chakravartî (second half of the sixteenth century), the writer who was called "the Jewel of Poets." He wrote a long narrative poem, the *Kavikankan-Chandî*, in honor of the Goddess; his language is vigorous and his descriptions of Bengal in his own day are precious to us in ours. His popularity can be compared with that of Tulsîdâs in Hindî territory. This literary vein continues into the eighteenth century, when it is represented by two much-prized *shakta* poets. The first of these is Bhâratchandra (1712-60), a Brâhman of Basantapur, principally remembered as having written a *mangala* or "poem of glorification" to Annadâ, the Goddess conceived as "giver of nourishment"; this is a collection of legends, into which the poet weaves a secular romantic epic (the *Vidyâsundara*) and a pseudo-historical novel. The style is scholarly and full of virtuosity. To the same writer we also owe a treatise on poetics *(Rasamañjari),* and a play *(Chandînâtaka)* written in a mixture of Sanskrit, Bengali and Persian.

His rival was Râmprasâd Sen (1718-78), of the caste of the *vaidakyas,* who wrote numerous poems to the "Divine Mother." He, of all the poets devoted to the worship of Kâlî, is the one who is closest to the people; his religious emotion, imbued with fear and humility, is vigorous and sincere. Even today, these naïve songs can be heard in any Bengal village.

The modern period is particularly important in Bengal; it has been specially characterized by the influence of other literatures. It is usually agreed that the period began with the career of Râmmohan RâY (1772-1833).[5] His early preoccupations were religious: he wanted to reform Hinduism by means of a return to Vedic tradition (he translated the *Upanishads* into English), and thus to lay the foundations of a purified faith that would be morally irreproachable and universally acceptable. He founded the Brâhmasamâj and poured out his ideas in propaganda pamphlets in which he also embarked on social and educational themes. He had an easy, fluent prose style well adapted to polemical purposes. From his lifetime on, social themes dominated literature in Bengal to a greater extent than in any other part of India. This predominance is partly due to the fact that Bengal has been specially receptive to Western influences: chiefly to English sociologists and romantic writers, but also, through English translations, to French writers such as Hugo, Michelet, Comte and Renan.

Bengali drama is partly popular in origin, as can be seen in the *yâtras,* melodramas, the declaiming of which is an accessory to processions and pilgrimages. The subjects of *yâtras* are drawn

[5] Renou, *The Nature of Hinduism,* chap. viii.

from the worship of Krishna or Râma or from one of the *shakta* cults, and the dramatic presentation is more or less naïve and rudimentary. A more modern tendency appears in the work of Râmnârâyan Tarkaratna, whose *Kulîndasarvasva* makes a violent attack on the polygamous Brâhmans (*kulînas*); while Dînabandhu Mitra, in his *Nîldarpana*, depicts the indigo plantation workers and their poverty. There are many plays reflecting similar tendencies; and, from the beginning of the nineteenth century, a large number of English plays, and other foreign plays in English translation, were translated into Bengali.

The most impressive poetry of the mid-nineteenth century is that of Michael Madhusûdan Datta (1824-73), a Hindu convert to Christianity. He is regarded as the renovator of Bengali epic writing because of his *Meghanâda-Vadha*, which describes an episode from the *Râmâyana*. He also tried to revive the Brajbulî lyric. He made use of the Western classics as well as the great works of Indian literature.

From this time on nationalistic feeling began to appear in literature. For example, there is the work of Bankimchandra Chattopâdhyâya (1838-94), who has been called "the father of the Bengali novel"; he was an imitator of Sir Walter Scott, using historical subjects but working social preoccupations into them at the same time. In his "Cloister of Felicity" (*Ânandamatha*) he describes the struggle of an ascetic order against both Moslems and British. He also wrote essays, one of which portrays an up-to-date Krishna who reasons like any positivist! In addition, he wrote the poem *Bande Mâtaram*, "I Hail the Mother," which later became the Indian national anthem.

The epics of Nabînchandra Sen (1846-1909), notably a vast trilogy that is a kind of parody of the *Mahâ-Bhârata*, show a dexterous handling of both legendary and historical subjects; and his novel *Bhânumatî* was widely read at one time. He, too, presented the world with a modern, progressive Krishna.

Of the poets, the most noteworthy is Dvijendralâl RâУ

(1864-1913), with his impeccably constructed social and historical plays and patriotic poems.

But of course the name that not only dominates recent Bengali literature but is also the best-known literary name in modern India as a whole, is that of Tagore (Rabîndranâth Thâkur, Anglicized to "Tagore"), 1861-1941. He was descended from a rich Bengali family (which had come from Oudh in the distant past and which claimed an eighth-century Sanskrit dramatist, Bhatta-Nârâyana, as a member of its ancestral line); his grandfather Dvârkanâth, and his father Debendranâth, "the *maharshi*," had played an important part in the Brâhmasamâj movement. Young Tagore studied in England and began writing in literary reviews as soon as he returned to Bengal; an early work, published under a pseudonym, was the imitation of the old Brajbuli lyric, some unpublished stanzas of which he said he had rediscovered. Fame came to him when he was hailed as a great poet by a group of English writers, the sequel being that he was awarded the Nobel Prize in 1913. He went back to Europe several times, visited Japan and the United States, and for a while played an active part in politics. But the major event in his life, outside his literary work, was the founding of a kind of university (the Vishvabhâratî) at Sântiniketan ("the home of peace"), in 1921, just as his grandfather had founded an *âshrama* in 1863, and his father a school in 1901. Tagore, following the example of the "hermitages" of ancient times, organized an eclectic education, in communion with nature and based on a broad humanism in which Eastern and Western values were harmoniously blended.

Moreover his whole literary work, which was extensive, was aimed at gainsaying Kipling's pronouncement that "East is East, and West is West, and never the twain shall meet." Tagore believed in this meeting and urged its consummation on the cultural level, in the setting provided by a spiritual life that involved no formal membership in any religious body, but that drew on the living forces of nature and of India's traditions. He felt he had a mission in this respect, and he was faithful to his mission to the end.

The essential, most characteristic part of his work as a writer is lyrical. The subject matter and impact of his poems are different at different stages in his career: there are pure lyrics ("The Golden Boat," "Beauty," "The Harvest"); love poems ("The Gardener"); poems with a pantheistic tendency, notably *Gîtânjali* (1913; translated as "A Lyrical Offering"), his masterpiece, inspired to some extent by ancient India; "The Basket of Fruit"; children's plays ("The Young Moon"); and mystical plays ("The Fugitive"). There are also didactic poems, and adaptations of folk poetry and ancient legends, and translations from Kabîr. Several volumes were translated into English by the poet himself, but the original version is far superior—if only by reason of its delicate rhythms and apt rhymes, and also a diction that is too fluid and vague by Western standards but that has its charms when one reads it as an Indian would.

Tagore's dramas are first cousins to his poetry; they are dramatically weak, being not so much plays as lyrical recitatives. They include "Nature's Revenge" *(Prakritî-Pratishodh)*; *Sannyâsî* (known in Europe as "The Ascetic"), which shows that a man's salvation lies in communion with nature, not in withdrawal from the world; "The Waterfall" *(Muktadhârâ),* depicting the clash between national interests and human brotherhood; "The King of the Black Room" (the title in Bengali is simply *Râjâ),* a kind of allegory reflecting the relationship between the Godhead and the individual soul; and *Dâkghar* ("The Post Office"), the story of an invalid boy who watches the world from his bed and is feverishly waiting for a reply to the letter he has written to the king.

Tagore's prose works are past numbering: stories of various kinds, tales for children and grownups, critical and philosophical essays (such as *Sâdhanâ,* or "Realization," "the religion of man"), social propaganda, political and religious writings, speeches, letters, reminiscences. Much is still unpublished.

In spite of their obvious imperfections it is impossible to overlook some of his novels, such as "The Shipwreck," *Gorâ* (the best of them) and "The House and the World." The influence of Western poetry on Tagore, which sets us a critical problem, is plausible on a priori grounds, and indeed probable in the case of Browning and some others; but whatever he took from the West he vigorously rethought and "Indianized."

Coming to more recent generations, a position of special distinction must be allotted to Saratchandra Chatterji (Chattopâdhyâya) (b. 1876), a novelist with an enormous public. He shows profound sympathy for human wretchedness; at the same time his faith in the future is not overlaid by the somewhat gloomy realism of his social observation. In *Srikanta* he embarks on his favorite theme, the attitude of society toward the woman of professionally light morals.

The poet Nazrul (Kazi Nazrul Islam) aims at delivering a message intended not only for his coreligionists, the Moslems of Bengal, but for every Indian.

Manik Banerji (Bandyopâdhâya), Tarasankar and "Bana Phul" are prose writers who have distinguished themselves in several fields.

"The Harvest" *(Navanna)*, a drama by Bijon Bhattacharya and Shambu Mitra, which vividly describes the life of the Bengal peasants during the last famine, attracted much attention.

Literature on technical and professional subjects is well represented: no province can boast scholars of more brilliant abilities than Bengal. Finally, in the field of homiletics, mention must be made of the maxims and parables of a great mystic, Ramakrishna, which have been collected by his disciples. His style is simple but frequently striking, and not devoid of humor.[6]

---

[6] Renou, *The Nature of Hinduism,* chap. viii.

It is clear that Bengali literature is the most abundant and varied of contemporary Indian literatures, and perhaps the most important. It is certainly the one that has most often been translated into Western languages; the works of Tagore, in particular, have excited intense curiosity and have attracted attention to other Bengali writers in consequence. The Bengali language has the reputation of being specially musical and, in poetry, capable of the subtlest modulations.

Singhalese

The literature of Ceylon has always stood, and still stands, quite outside the main currents of Indian literature. Singhalese is an aberrant Indo-European language—of "colonial" type, as some have called it—and was influenced by a Tamil substratum. Old Singhalese, in which the "classical" literature is written, is called *elu*. It is exclusively Buddhist, consisting chiefly of translations, paraphrases, commentaries on Pâli texts, and annals recording the history of Buddhist communities in Ceylon. Most of the works belong to the thirteenth and fourteenth centuries, one of the earliest being the *Amâvatura* of Gurulugomi, a collection of the Buddha's discourses and dialogues. The poetry stems from the *Jâtakas* and is mostly written in scholarly style.

In the fifteenth century a slightly more secular tendency arises. The dominant feature is the rise of the genre known as *sandesha*, or "message," the best specimen of which is the "Message of the *Maina* Bird," by Totagamuva (Shrî-Râhula Thera); the same writer also composed a *Kâvyashekhara*, a poem in *Mahâkâvya* style, based on one of the *Jâtakas*.

In the seventeenth century there was a new surge of writing in the form of parables and maxims, and, more notably, a version of the *Kusajâtaka* in six hundred and eighty-seven stanzas, by Alagiyavanna Mukaveti (who was converted to

Christianity). Technical compositions included grammars, lexicons, works on poetics, history and other subjects.

Contemporary Singhalese literature is fairly rich in popular poetry, mostly of a Buddhist tendency; there are also epics on local legends, one of which, though called a *Jâtaka*, is really an imitation of a Tamil version of the *Mahâ-Bhârata*. There are work songs, play songs and dancing songs, and poems about the struggle against the Portuguese and the British.

Finally, a small "modern" literature has sprung up under the influence of English literary models. Among the names in this quarter are Kumaranatunga, who is a critic, Tennakoon, a poet who writes *sandeshas*, and Matin Wickremasinghe, a novelist.

Indian Writers in English

Due honor must be paid here to those Indians who have chosen English as their medium of expression. First, the scholars: for the last hundred years most Indian works of serious scholarship have been written in English. To mention only two such writers, both of whom stand out on account of their brilliant style, S. K. De, of Dacca, has studied the history of Sanskrit literature and of the Indian religions; and the philosopher S. Radhakrishnan, a Tamil by birth, has worked on the history of philosophy, has distinguished himself as an orator, and is a dazzling manipulator of ideas.

Politicians, whenever they seek an all-Indian hearing (and especially if they want a hearing outside India as well), express themselves in English. Such a one is Prime Minister Jawaharlâl Nehru (born in Kashmir), a brilliant orator, like Radhakrishnan, and a writer of vigorous English.

There are also the spiritual writers—such as the ardent and sometimes profound Vivekânanda (late nineteenth century), a Bengali by birth, a disciple of Râmakrishna, and the creator of

Neo-Vedântism.[7] Another and more recent example is the "sage of Pondicherry," Aurobindo Ghose (also a Bengali),[8] who wrote poems as well as religious works.

In this category (of Indian writers using English) we may also group those Indians, such as Tagore, who have translated some of their own works into English.

Tagore's name brings us to poetry. Henry Derozio (early nineteenth century) was a Eurasian who died very young; his verse is delicate and passionate; like John Ricketts, he preached the cause of Anglo-Indian unity. Later in the century come the sisters Toru and Aru Dutt, whose exceptional poetic gifts attracted the attention of Edmund Gosse. Toward the end of the century Manmohan Ghose (Aurobindo's brother) wrote his love songs and elegies, which have a sharp nostalgia. Ananda Coomaraswamy, a Singhalese, known principally as an art historian and the pioneer of a kind of comparative mysticism, also wrote interesting poems. But in the present day the name to be remembered above all is that of Sarojinî Naidu (Bengal), whose poems reveal an acute sense both of Indian life and of nature; "the Mîrâbâî of today," as Gandhi used to call her. A writer whose position is somewhat apart, but who must not be omitted, is Romesh Chunder Dutt (Bengal), who has been indefatigable as a translator of the Epics. Mention must also be made of the writings in English of Madhusûdan Datta.

In prose, the most widely known name is that of Dhan Gopal Mukerji (Bengal), with his children's stories, his autobiography (*My Brother's Face*), his vibrant essay on Râmakrishna (*The Face of Silence*), and his observations on the United States, in which he lived for years (*Brahman and Outcast*). In a later generation, the Panjâbî Mulk Raj Ânand is a brilliant essayist, and his novel *Coolie* won considerable success in the West. Among the writers in Tamil two outstanding

---

[7] Renou, *The Nature of Hinduism*, chap. viii.
[8] Ibid., chap. viii.

names are K. S. Venkataramani, poet and novelist, and R. K. Narayan, a novelist and writer of short stories.

There is considerable activity in the way of literary periodicals in English. The future of Indian literature in English is of course precarious; but at least Indians can be proud of its achievements so far; it bears witness to the exceptional facility that many of them possess for absorbing an alien language, even in its furthest and most subtle reaches.

APPENDIX

Indian Literature and the West

The direct, massive expansion of Indian thought—through Sanskrit literature, and also through Pâli—took place during the first millennium A.D., in the direction of East Asia: reaching as far as the outer limits of Indonesia, and to Japan, and also northward to Tibet, eastern Turkestan and Mongolia. It is essentially a matter of Buddhist doctrines and legends: a considerable part of Buddhist literature, lost in India itself, can be more or less exactly reconstituted with the help of the translations that were made in various Asiatic languages. But Buddhism was not the only factor at work: Brahmanic texts and Hindu teachings, sometimes carried by Buddhism and sometimes traveling independently, also penetrated as far as the fringes of the Pacific: legends of Râma and the heroes of the Mahâ-Bhârata, myths of the Hindu deities, the doctrines of *dharma* (especially the *Laws of Manu*) and those of the *Âyur-Veda,* and others too. The whole phenomenon is of primary historical importance; no expansion on a similar scale can be found save that of Christianity in the West.

The influence of Indian thought on Europe has, certainly, been much less profound. But it is far from negligible; it has not been (as some people have too readily believed) limited to a tinge of exoticism here and there in the nineteenth-century poetry and painting, or to some ill-defined smattering of theosophy.

We must begin at the beginning—which means in ancient Greek times. In Herodotus first, and later in Ctesias, Greece had writers who were eager to note stange customs and who prepared the ground for the mythical picture of "India the land of wonders." But the Greeks were also curious for ideas. Religious and philosophical conceptions from India, no doubt through Iranian or Asiatic intermediaries, made their way into Greece at an early period. It has often been conceded that Plotinus and the Neoplatonist milieu had been in contact with ancient Vedântic thought, that is to say, with the content of the Vedic *Upanishads.*

Contact ceased during the Middle Ages. News of India reached the West only with occasional travelers as the centuries rolled on—the most famous being Marco Polo, in the thirteenth century. The tales, the *fabliaux*—the whole tradition of storytelling, written or spoken, that reached its European destination in Grimm and Andersen, after passing through a multitude of intermediate versions, illustrious or obscure, on the way—go back partly to Indian subjects and models: the *Jâtakas* and the *Pañchatantra.* But this ultimate source was lost to mind, and La Fontaine[1] knew only by hearsay, and in a mangled form at that, the name of the "Indian sage" from whose stories his fables were in fact derived.

A very few Sanskrit texts started to become known in the seventeenth century, thanks to missionaries from various European countries. In the eighteenth century that admirable explorer and scholar, Anquetil Duperron, set sail for Bombay,

---

[1] Jean de la Fontaine (1621-95), whose *Fables* are the masterpiece of a great poet. The "Indian sage" was "Pilpay" (really Bidpai), whose tales La Fontaine had read in a contemporary rendering of a Persian translation. —TR.

intent on discovering the Holy Scriptures of India and Persia. He found only part of them, but he did obtain a Persian translation of the *Upanishads* and prepared a Latin version of it, which in due course was read with passionate interest by Schopenhauer.[2] The eighteenth century came close to unveiling the "mystery" of ancient India. Even Voltaire, with his polemical, skeptical attitude, helped rather than hindered the scholars' endeavors.

But it was in Germany, during the last quarter of the eighteenth century, that a receptive state of mind was created for ideas from the inaccessible East. Herder launched the idea (the illusion, rather) of primitive poetry; Goethe had something like a premonition of the great Oriental texts, and enthusiastically hailed the first translation of *Shakuntala* (by Sir William Jones, 1789).

This was the period at which the decisive factor began to operate: the deciphering and publication of the earliest Sanskrit texts by Western scholars who were in touch with Indian *panditas* (pundits). This was the beginning of what R. Schwab has justly called the Oriental Renaissance: just as the humanistic sixteenth century had rediscovered classical antiquity, so the late eighteenth century rediscovered the East and the wonders of Indian thought. The first Asiatic Society was founded in 1784, in Calcutta. One after the other the great texts emerged from the shadows; in several countries, writers seized on Indian ideas and images almost as soon as they had been put into circulation. In Germany, Goethe followed Herder, and Novalis and Jean-Paul Richter joined the pursuit in their turn, while the brothers Schlegel, with their critical authority, played the part of mediators between the educated public and the small, enclosed world of the scholars.

It was from 1830 to 1860, or later, that India's invasion of European literature went forward most vigorously. After the

---

[2] Readers of Schopenhauer's *magnum opus, The World as Will and Idea,* will remember the respect with which he speaks of Hindu philosophy. —Tr.

Bhagavad-Gîtâ and the *Upanishads,* the Veda itself was edited and translated; then came the Great Epic, tales, court poetry, several of the great Hindu and Buddhist texts, and the monumental works in law, medicine and philosophy.

In France, where the Société Asiatique was founded in 1822, a little before its counterpart in London, and where the first chair of Sanskrit studies was set up at the Collège de France as early as 1814, it is surprising to see how many writers of the first prominence were attracted to ancient India. Among the poets there were Vigny, Victor Hugo and, especially, Lamartine; among the historians, Michelet and Quinet; among the scientists, Cuvier and Ampère; not to mention seekers after the exotic, such as Théophile Gautier. The salons played a part in the craze. Certain amateurs hungry for erudition, such as the "Baron" d'Eckstein, developed nothing less than a vocation for Orientalism. In Italy the name of Leopardi is the most noteworthy in this connection.

In Germany, where the movement had started earlier, it continued into the romantic epoch. More than the poets (among whom we must at least mention Rückert, with his genius for translation) and the historians, it was the philosophers who were most affected by it at first; the influence starts with Kant, goes on to Schopenhauer and Hartmann, and includes Hegel and Schelling. In the Anglo-Saxon countries it affected essayists, such as Carlyle and Emerson, and also poets. Certainly, in the case of a Shelley or a Wordsworth, it was not so much a matter of influence as of coincidence, and, at times, of an echo of Neoplatonic ideas. All the poets' names ought to be quoted here, from Coleridge to Browning, whose Vedântic inspiration has been pointed out a number of times. For, indeed, what great poet, if once he turns in the direction of pantheism and allows his mind to be charmed by the appeal of mystical forces, does not become more or less "Indian," that is to say, unconsciously in communion with the thought of ancient India?

True, there were some dissenting voices. In France, Voltaire's irony was repeated and prolonged in the detached attitude of Jacquemont. In Britain, the "Anglo-Indian" writers retained their nostalgia for the West, and showed a lack of love and a distrust toward India that sometimes developed into actual hostility. Under a host of surface variations it was this attitude, toward the end of the century, that characterized Kipling, whose British or Anglo-Indian heroes are very conscious of their racial superiority.

After 1860, Western interest in India, though no less profound than before, assumed more moderate forms for the most part. Scholarship had given rise to a more prudent approach. Taine and Renan examined Buddhism and Indian thought in general with a critical sense that, though sympathetic, was alert. Others, such as Gobineau, writing in a not altogether impartial spirit, drew attention to the "Vedic Aryans" (as the expression went) as evidence for the theory of racial inequality. Wagner in his late period comes in here; so does Nietzsche, who was indebted to India for his ideas on the "eternal return," his aspirations toward a superhuman life,[3] and his perhaps pessimistic view of history and the modern world.

The poets of the post-romantic period remained faithful to India, though they cannot always be acquitted of the charge of exoticism: Leconte de Lisle in France (Mallarmé, too, with his *Contes Indiens);* Carducci *(Odi Barbari)* in Italy; Stefan George in Germany; Edwin Arnold in England; Gjellerup in Denmark; Whitman in America; Maeterlinck in Belgium. At the other end of Europe, Tolstoy rediscovered Indian "non-violence," finding himself thoroughly at home with themes that are part of the Indian spiritual tradition at all periods of its history.

It is difficult to give a concise picture of the complex tendencies that attract so many minds toward India today. Let us try to situate in their appropriate place (which is certainly not the leading one) the labors of orientalists, ever concerned to strengthen the objective foundations on which their studies are based: chronology, history, philology, historical connections between one doctrine and another—those guides that are indispensable if knowledge is not to go astray. To consider Sanskrit alone, we are faced not with the few dozen texts that were known a hundred years ago, but with the ten thousand and more that have now been listed and described. There is no common measure between even the most modest endeavors in present-day oriental scholarship, and the fantasies, however brilliant they may be, that amateurs throw off so easily and in such plenty.

There has been a profusion of books about India, but not many of them can boast any more durable feature than the literary success that in some cases their authors' talent has won for them. Among the few exceptions are *In India,* by Hermann Hesse, *A Passage to India,* by E. M. Forster, and *An Indian Day,* by Edward Thompson. Some degree of access to Yoga is made possible by the work of Paul Brunton, which, in a realm abounding in charlatanism, can be recommended with more confidence than any others.[4] Keyserling's *Travel Diary of a Philosopher* makes a not unsuccessful attempt to interpret Indian doctrines as a function of Indian life and culture. Lanza del Vasto's *Pilgrimage to the Sources* is not specially attractive; but *Un Barbare en Asie,* by Henri Michaux, despite its deliberate absurdities of expression, is rewarding and suggestive.

Poetry is another of the means through which our contact with India is maintained. The Irish writers A. E. (George William Russell) and William Butler Yeats, whose work echoes the nostalgia of romanticism, were captivated by India; it was Yeats who brought about the West's discovery of Tagore. The only event that can be compared with Tagore's emergence in the Western firmament is the impact made in the twenties by the ideas of Gandhi, an event at once spiritual and political. In France, André Gide and Pierre-Jean Jouve were the pioneers in spreading Tagore's message, and Gide, in his preface to *Gîtâñjali,* points out in how profound a degree Tagore's writing

[4] Perhaps a word should be said for *Yoga: The Method of Re-Integration,* by Alain Daniélou (New York: Wehman Bros.) This is directly based throughout on Sanskrit texts, whose originals are quoted in an Appendix. There is also an erudite study, not a practical manual, by Mircéa Eliade, *Yoga: Immortality and Freedom,* tr. Willard R. Trask (New York: Pantheon Books, 1958).—Tr.

was inspired by the forms and content of Vedic literature. T. S. Eliot has felt the attraction of India: *The Fire Sermon* and *What The Thunder Said,* in *The Waste Land,* are partly built, respectively, on a Buddhist parable and reminiscences of the *Upanishads.* To return to France, both René Daumal and Simone Weil studied Sanskrit grammar and Indian poetics and doctrines. On the other hand, if Jacquemont in the romantic period failed to understand India, an even clumsier and more thorough failure in our own period is that of Claudel, who perpetuated the morbid confusion into which matters had been thrown by Henri Massis.

It need hardly be repeated that, in the West's concern with India, the dominating quest is the spiritual one. The Hollywood school is an Indianized mystical circle, one of whose adherents is Aldous Huxley. The ironist of *Jesting Pilate* is now a convert to the delusive phantoms of the *philosophia perennis;* his anthology, *The Perennial Philosophy,* is lavishly garnished with quotations from Sanskrit. Christopher Isherwood has collaborated with a swami to produce a poetic paraphrase of the *Gita* and has published some of his own studies under the title *Vedânta for the Western World.* The American school endeavors to rediscover a kind of primitive tradition; this is also the objective of René Guénon, who has studied Shankaryan *Vedânta* at second hand and written a book about it. The brilliant Americanized Indian Coomaraswamy, with his interpretation of Indian mythology, gave the school a framework within which to build. *India Invades America* was the title of a book by Wendell Thomas in 1930.

In Germany, where a process of semi-scholarly inquiry has been pushed forward by Keyserling (already mentioned), and Spengler and Max Weber, and where R. Otto's studies in comparative mysticism have unleashed an interest in Brahmanic philosophy, it is nevertheless Buddhism that occupies the center of the stage—first of all, with such a figure as the proselyte K. E. Neumann, the translator of the sermons of "Gotamo Buddho," and later with G. Grimm, and A. Güth, who became the *bhikku*

Nyânatiloka. Nearer at hand, Albert Schweitzer has stressed (but excessively) that negation of the will-to-live which in his eyes contains the essence of post-Upanishadic philosophy. But it is Romain Rolland more than anyone else who has been responsible for the propagation in Europe of what can be called neo-Hinduism. Rolland assisted this cause with all the weight of his literary prestige and lyrical power. His well-informed books on Râmakrishna and Vivekânanda have provoked several other writers into providing an eager public with a plentiful flow of studies and translations. We can watch this neo-Hinduism, which came to birth in the life and writings of Râmmohan Râly, reaching its consummation and its end in the work of Aurobindo Ghose, whose work is beginning to make itself felt in the West. It was by Rolland that Bergson (in his *Two Sources of Morality and Religion)* was led to compare Indian and Christian mysticism, deciding in favor of the second—but, in doing so, showing perhaps more gravity of demeanor than weight of argument.

This neo-Hinduism, whatever compromises it has been compelled to make with Western values, is at least authentically Indian. The same cannot be said of theosophy, which, since Mme. Blavatsky and her book *The Secret Doctrine* (1888), has been drawing upon Indian religiosity and cosmology to create what R. Kanters has described as a kind of spiritual, and spiritualistic, evolutionism.

Looking at the whole question of Eastern influence on the West, it is difficult and doubtless impossible to distinguish between real and as it were textual influences, and the much more frequent occurrence of affinity and convergence. This convergence has been detected, rightly or wrongly, from Plotinus to Herder and from Lamartine to Bergson. Among the moderns it can be seen in Proust and in Morgan; in Thomas Mann, who tried to produce a kind of imitation Hindu legend in *The Transposed Heads*; and in D. H. Lawrence, who, however, could see nothing in present-day India but decadence and barbarism.

What people seek from India is, at bottom, what they possess in themselves, what they have already found. India is an alibi, the mythical setting in which a certain literary esotericism achieves its fulfillment. India has indeed had her own share of genuine esotericism; occult correspondences and analogies have been part of her culture from the beginning. But the movements created in Europe, though claiming that their authority comes from her, are rarely a faithful reflection. No real yogin and no traditionally inclined Indian would find his proper nourishment among them. One must make up one's mind to it: Indian spirituality (to quote a saying that has been both used and abused) is not designed for export. It is the result of intimate experience, and of experiment even more than of speculative thought; it is a whole, and can be understood only if considered as a whole.

The alternative, for those unwilling to follow the path of erudition (a hard path, but the only useful and fruitful one), is to seek intoxication from a kind of mystical exoticism, as was done in romantic times; to muse about cosmogonies and myths; to imagine a universe explicable on monistic and pantheistic lines (a pan-entheistic universe, as it has been more accurately called). Such visions may be exalting; they may even be a stimulus to artistic creation. But it must be clearly recognized that the reality of India is barely touched by these all too summary daydreams.

What would have been desirable, on a more real, positive plane, is that India should have been fully integrated into the wider humanism that we can see being worked out before us today.

BRIEF CHRONOLOGY

Note: Where ancient times are concerned, most of the dates given are hypothetical in varying degree.

25th-20th cent. Indus civilizations (Mohenjo-Daro).	
20th-15th cent.	*Rig-Veda.*
15th cent. Bhârata war (according to the *Purânas*).	
14th cent. Parîkshit	*Atharva-Veda.*
13th cent. Yâjñavalkya	*White Yajur-Veda.*
11th-9th cent.	*Shatapatha-Brâhmana.*
8th-5th cent.	Principal *Upanishads;* principal Vedic *Sûtras.*
558. Birth of Buddha	
486. Ajâtashatru, king of Magadha.	
478. Death of Buddha.	
	Pânini. Definitive form of the *Mahâ-Bhârata* begins taking shape.
327. Alexander's invasion.	
313. Chandragupta (Maurya dynasty).	
	Original nucleus of the *Kautiliya.*
264. Asoka	Inscriptions of Ashoka.

226. Death of Asoka

Definitive form of the *Râmayana* begins taking shape.

189. Invasion of Demetrios.

Definitive form of Pâli Canon.

176. The Shungas.
168. Menander (Milinda) in Panjâb.
1st cent. . . . .

Mahâ-Bhâshya.
Laws of Manu.

90. Invasion of the Shakas ("Indo-Scythians").
70. The Shâtavâhanas.
A.D. 30. The Kushânas.

Definitive form of the *Jâtakas.*
Earliest philosophical *Sûtras.*
Nâtya-Shâstra.
Smriti of Yâjñavalkya.
Definitive form of the medical *Samhitâs.*

2nd cent. . . . .

144. Accession of Kanishka.

Nâgârjuna; Ashvaghosa; Hâla.
Smriti of Vishnu.
Early examples of *Sangam* (Tam.).
Kundakunda.

245. End of the great Kushânas.

Smriti of Nârada.
Definitive form of the principal *Purânas.*

320. Chandragupta I (Gupta dynasty).
Early Vâkâtakas (Deccan).

Kâma-Sûtras.

335. Death of Chandragupta I; Samudragupta.
The Pallavas.

Mricchakatikâ.
Anthology "of Hâla"; comedies "of Bhasa."

375. Death of Samudragupta; Chandragupta II.

Kâlidâsa; Amarasimha.

388. End of Shaka rule in India.

414. Death of Chandragupta II;
Kumâragupta I.

Buddhaghosa; Assanga.

450. Hephtalite invasions.
The Kadambas.
455. Death of Kumaragupta I;
Skandagupta.

Vasubandhu.

485. Toramâna in Mâlava.

Kural (Tam.).

500. Western Câlukyas. End of
the Vâkâtakas.

Brihat-Samhitâ.

510. Gupta empire dismembered.

Bhâravi.

533. Yashodharman;
defeat of Mihirakula.
550. End of the Hephtalites.
Pulakeshin I (Vâtâpi dy-
nasty).
566. Death of Pulakeshin I.

Dandin; Chandragomin.

605. Harshavardhana.
609. Pulakeshin II.

Comedies of Harsha.
Mâgha; Bâna; Bhartrihari.

625. The Pallavas.
629. Hiuan-tsang begins his
travels.

Dharmakirtî; Chantideva.
Nammâlvâr (Tam.).

642. End of Hiuan-tsang's
travels.
Death of Pulakeshin II.
647. Death of Harshavardhana.

Mânikkavâsagar (Tam.).

671-95. Travels of Yi-tsing.

Kumârila.
Bhavabhûti; Vâgbhata.

753. The Râshtrakûtas
(Mahârâshtra).

Haribhadra.

760. The Pâlas (Bengal).

Tirumangai (Tam.).

775. Apogee of the power of the
     Pratihâras (Gurjaras).
     (Râjputânâ).

Shankara.

836. Bhoja I of Kanauj.
850. The Colas.

Vâcaspamishra; Râjashekhara.

880. The Kalachuris
     (Haihayas).
892. Eastern Châlukyas
     (Bhîma I).
900. The Paramaras (Mâlva).

Pampa (Kann.); Pushpadanta.
Chintâmani (Tam.);
     Somadevasûri.

962. Foundation of the Kingdom
     of Ghaznî.
973. The Châlukyas of Kalyâni.
985. Râjarâja the Great (Cola).

Têvâram (Tam.); *Nâlâyiram*
     (Tam.).
Abhinavagupta; Udayana.

997. Mahmûd sultan of Ghaznî.
1012. Rajendra I (Cola).
1018. Kanauj captured by
      Mahmûd.
1030. Death of Mahmûd.
1044. Death of Rajendra I.

Katharitsagara.

1070. Kulottunga I (Cola).

Bilhana; Râmânuja.

1090. The Gâhadavâlas (U.P.).
1100. The Senas (Bengal).
1106. The Hoysalas (Mysore).

Vijñâneshvara.

1122. Death of Kulottunga I.
1143-72. Kumârapâla (Gujrât).

Kalhana; Hemachandra;
     Bhaskâra.
Basava (Kann.).
Jayadeva.

1175. Muhammad Ghori's
      invasion.

1178. Kulottunga III (Cola).

    Kamban (Tam.); Shriharsha.

1185. Lakshmanasena (Bengal).
1190. Apogee of the power of the
    Yâdavas (Mahârâshtra).
1192. Capture of Delhi; fall of
    the Châhamânas
    (Chauhâns).
1194. Fall of the Gâhadavâlas.
1200. Death of Lakshmanasena;
    end of the Pâlas and the
    Senas.

    Maykandâr (Tam.).

1206. Death of Muhammad Ghori.
1220. Pândya hegemony begins.
1221. First Mongol invasions.

    Madhva.

1266. Balban.

    Tikkana (Tel.); Nimbârka;
    Nâmdev (Mar.).

1279. End of the Cola dynasty.
1287. Death of Balban.
1290. Turkish dynasty of the
    Khaljîs (Firûz I).

    Completion of the *Jnaneshvari*
    (Mar.).

1292-93. Marco Polo in southern
    India.
1297. Conquest of Gujrât.
1302. Capture of Chitôr.

    Vedântadeshika.

1305. Delhi captured by the
    Khaljîs.
1317. End of the Yâdavas.
1320. The Tughlaks.
1325. Tughlak II (Muhammad
    bin Tughluq).
1327. End of the Hoysalas.
1336. Founding of Vijayanagar.

    Mâdhava.

1347. The Bahmanîs (Deccan).
1351. Death of Tughlak II;
    Firûz III.
1388. Death of Firûz III
    and end of the Tughlaks.

1398. Invasions of Timur
(Tamerlane); sack of Delhi.

Chandidâs (Beng.); Vidyâpati
(Bih.).

1451. The Lodîs (Delhi).

Pôtana (Tel.); Vêmana (Tel.);
Kabîr (Hind.).

1494. Bâbur.

Nânak (Hind.); Chaitanya
(Beng.).

1518. End of the Bahmanis.

Vallabha; Sûrdâs (Hind.).

1526. Victory of Bâbur at
Pânipat, and end of the
Lodîs.
1530. Death of Bâbur; Humâyûn.
1537. Death of Bahâdur Shâh
(Gujrât).

Mîrâbâî (Hind.); Tulsidâs
(Hind.).
Madhusûdana; Vijnanabhikshu.

1556. Death of Humâyûn; Akbar.
1565. Battle of Talikota; end of
Vijayanagar.

Mukundaram (Beng.);
Appayadîkshita.
Keshavdâs (Hind.); Eknâth
(Mar.).

1605. Death of Akbar; Jahângir.

Tukârâm (Mar.).

1627. Death of Jahângir.
1628. Shâh Jahân.
1658. Aurangzeb.
1664. Beginning of the Mahratta
conquests.
Formation of East India
Company.
1674. Coronation of Shivâjî.
1675. Govind Singh.
1680. Death of Shîvajî.

Walî (Urdu).

1707. Death of Aurangzeb.
1708. Death of Govind Singh.

1742. Dupleix governor of
Pondicherry.
1744-1748. First Anglo-French
War.

Bhâratchandra (Beng.).

1756. Beginning of second Anglo-
French War.
1757. Battle of Plassey.
1758. Clive first governor
of Bengal.
1761. Fall of Pondicherry.

Râmprasâd Sen (Ben.);
Moropant (Mar.).

1767. Beginning of the wars of
Mysore.
1775-82. First Anglo-Mahratta
War.

Râmmohan Rây (Beng).

1803. Delhi occupied by the
British; Second Anglo-
Mahratta War.

Lallû Lâl (Hind.).

1817-19. Third Anglo-Mahratta
War.
1839-42. First Anglo-Afghan
War.
1845-49. Anglo-Sikh Wars.

Madhusûdan (Beng.);
Dayânand (Hind.).

1857. Indian Mutiny.
1877. Queen Victoria proclaimed
Empress of India.
1878-80. Second Anglo-Afghan
War.
1885. Indian National Congress
founded.

Hâli (Urdu); Bankimchandra
(Beng.).
Nabîn Sen (Beng.).
Tagore's career begins (Beng.).
Vivekânanda (Beng.).
Tilak (Mar.).
Premchand (Hind.); Iqbâl
(Urdu.).

1920. Gandhi President of
Congress.

Munchi (Guj.); Saratchandra
Chatterji (Beng.).
Aurobindo (Beng.).

1930. Civil Disobedience
Movement; Round Table
Conference.
1947. Independence proclaimed;
Nehru Prime Minister.
1948. Death of Gandhi.
1950. Proclamation of the Indian
Republic.

BIBLIOGRAPHY

General

The collection *The Indian Literatures* (Bombay; P.E.N. All-India Centre, 1941-), published in short separate volumes, would be useful if it were complete; but so far only a small part of the whole scheme has appeared.

Sanskrit

Of all the Indian literatures, Sanskrit is the one that has been by far the best and the one most often described. The principal recent or relatively recent works are M. Winternitz, *History of Indian Literature* (3 vols.; Leipzig, 1905-20; in German; the first two volumes and the first half of the third volume are also available in English translation); A. B. Keith, *A History of Sanskrit Literature* (N. Y.: Oxford U. P., 1928), which should be supplemented by the same author's *The Sanskrit Drama* (1924); and finally, the as yet unfinished *A History of Sanskrit Literature, Classical Period* (Vol. 1; Calcutta, 1947), by S. N. Dasgupta and S. K. De.

There are also plenty of shorter handbooks, especially in English, which need not be enumerated here.

Non-Sanskrit

Dinesh Chandra Sen, *History of Bengali Language and Literature* (Calcutta, 1911).

Contemporary

The Indian Literatures of Today: A Symposium (Bombay, 1947). (Somewhat disappointing).

BIBLIOGRAPHY

INDEX